Lith

Everything
Know

Introduction to Lithuania: A Baltic Gem

Nestled in the northeastern corner of Europe lies a hidden treasure waiting to be explored – Lithuania, a Baltic gem of unparalleled beauty and rich history. This enchanting country, often referred to as the "Land of a Thousand Lakes," offers a captivating blend of picturesque landscapes, vibrant culture, and a resilient spirit that has weathered centuries of trials and triumphs.

Lithuania, geographically situated on the eastern shore of the Baltic Sea, is the southernmost of the three Baltic states, sharing its borders with Latvia to the north, Belarus to the east, Poland to the southwest, and Russia's Kaliningrad Oblast to the west. With its strategic location, Lithuania has long been a crossroads of cultures and trade, contributing to its diverse heritage.

The story of Lithuania is one of endurance and resilience, marked by a storied past that has shaped its identity. Its origins can be traced back to the early Baltic tribes inhabiting the region, with the first recorded mention of the name "Lithuania" appearing in the 9th century. However, it wasn't until the late medieval period that Lithuania rose to prominence under the reign of Grand Duke Mindaugas, who established the Grand Duchy of Lithuania in the 13th century. This marked the beginning of Lithuania's ascendancy as a formidable power in Eastern Europe.

A pivotal moment in Lithuania's history came in 1386 when Grand Duke Jogaila (also known as Władysław II

Jagiełło) united the Grand Duchy of Lithuania with the Kingdom of Poland through the Union of Krewo. This union laid the foundation for a dynastic union, culminating in the formation of the Polish-Lithuanian Commonwealth, one of the largest and most influential states in Europe during the 16th and 17th centuries. This union not only shaped Lithuania's political landscape but also influenced its culture, introducing Catholicism and the Polish language.

Despite the challenges of foreign rule, Lithuania's indomitable spirit prevailed. In 1918, Lithuania reasserted its independence following World War I, becoming one of the first nations to break free from the disintegrating Russian Empire. The interwar period saw the country's rapid development, with its capital, Vilnius, emerging as a thriving cultural and intellectual center.

However, Lithuania's quest for freedom faced turbulent times during World War II and the subsequent Soviet occupation. The resilience of its people shone through during the Singing Revolution of the late 1980s, when mass protests and a human chain of unity, known as the Baltic Way, helped pave the way to independence from the Soviet Union. Lithuania reclaimed its sovereignty on March 11, 1990, and has since flourished as a sovereign nation, embracing its European identity and democratic principles.

Today, Lithuania stands as a testament to the enduring spirit of its people. Its capital, Vilnius, a UNESCO World Heritage site, boasts a charming old town with a mix of Baroque and Gothic architecture. The country's natural beauty is equally captivating, with pristine lakes, dense forests, and the mesmerizing Curonian Spit, a UNESCO-listed sand dune peninsula along the Baltic Sea.

Lithuania's rich cultural tapestry is woven with folklore, traditions, and a love for the arts. Its language, Lithuanian, one of the oldest living Indo-European languages, reflects a deep sense of national pride. The nation's love for music and dance is showcased in its vibrant festivals, while its culinary heritage, featuring hearty dishes like cepelinai (potato dumplings) and šaltibarščiai (cold beet soup), offers a taste of authentic Baltic flavors.

The Geographical Landscape of Lithuania

Lithuania's geographical landscape is a tapestry of natural beauty and diversity, offering a captivating blend of features that define this Baltic nation's character. Situated in the northeastern part of Europe, Lithuania stretches across approximately 65,300 square kilometers (25,200 square miles), making it the largest of the three Baltic states. Its unique geography plays a significant role in shaping the country's identity and its people's way of life.

At the heart of Lithuania lies a vast lowland region known as the Baltic Lowlands, which extends across the central and western parts of the country. This flat and fertile expanse is home to extensive forests, meadows, and numerous lakes, earning Lithuania its nickname as the "Land of a Thousand Lakes." These lakes, formed during the last Ice Age, create a picturesque mosaic that dots the landscape and offers ample opportunities for outdoor recreation and wildlife habitats.

The eastern part of Lithuania gradually gives way to more undulating terrain, marked by low hills and gently rolling landscapes. This region, known as the Baltic Uplands, adds depth and variety to the country's topography. Here, you'll find lush forests, fertile farmlands, and quaint villages nestled amidst the hills, providing a stark contrast to the flatlands of the west.

One of Lithuania's most iconic natural features is the Curonian Spit, a narrow and elongated sand dune peninsula that stretches along the southeastern shore of the Baltic Sea. Shared with Russia's Kaliningrad Oblast, this UNESCO World Heritage site boasts some of the tallest sand dunes in Europe. The Curonian Spit is a testament to the dynamic forces of nature, where wind and water constantly reshape the landscape. It's a haven for both nature enthusiasts and beachgoers, offering serene beaches on one side and dense pine forests on the other.

Lithuania's location along the southeastern coast of the Baltic Sea contributes to its maritime climate, characterized by mild summers and relatively cold winters. The Baltic Sea also plays a pivotal role in Lithuania's geography, influencing its weather patterns and providing access to trade routes and international commerce.

In the northern part of the country, you'll find the picturesque Žemaitija (Samogitian) Highlands, a region with more pronounced hills and valleys. This area showcases a different facet of Lithuania's natural beauty, with its scenic landscapes and charming villages.

Rivers also crisscross the Lithuanian terrain, with the Neris, Nemunas, and Venta rivers being some of the most significant. The Nemunas River, in particular, is the country's longest and serves as a vital waterway for transportation and trade.

Lithuania's geographical diversity has not only influenced its climate and natural features but has also shaped its cultural and historical development. The fertile lowlands have been essential for agriculture, while the dense forests provided timber resources. The country's numerous lakes and rivers have been sources of freshwater and fisheries, contributing to both sustenance and trade.

Ancient Origins: Lithuania's Early History

Lithuania's early history is a tale of ancient origins, a narrative that reaches deep into the annals of time. Long before written records, the land that is now Lithuania was inhabited by various Baltic tribes. These early inhabitants left behind traces of their existence, offering tantalizing glimpses into the region's prehistoric past.

Archaeological evidence suggests that human settlements in Lithuania date back to the Neolithic period, around 3000 BCE. The people of this era were skilled farmers and hunters who relied on the fertile soil and abundant natural resources of the region for their sustenance. Over time, these tribes developed a rich culture, crafting intricate pottery and decorative items.

As the centuries rolled on, the Bronze Age arrived in Lithuania, marked by the advent of metalworking. Bronze tools, ornaments, and weapons began to appear, showcasing the technological advancements of the time. The people of the region engaged in trade with neighboring cultures, exchanging goods and ideas.

The Iron Age followed, and it brought with it significant changes to the way of life in Lithuania. Iron tools and weapons became prevalent, enhancing agriculture and defense capabilities. The Iron Age also saw the emergence of fortified hillforts, strategically located settlements that served as centers of governance and protection.

During this period, the Baltic tribes inhabiting Lithuania began to organize themselves into cohesive tribal entities. They developed their own distinct cultures, languages, and traditions. While there is limited written documentation from this time, linguistic evidence suggests that the Lithuanian language, one of the oldest living Indo-European languages, was already in use.

The early history of Lithuania is intertwined with the broader context of the Baltic peoples, who inhabited a vast territory encompassing present-day Latvia, Estonia, and parts of northern Poland. These tribes shared cultural similarities but also had their unique identities.

It wasn't until the late 12th century that Lithuania began to take its first steps toward a more unified state. Under the leadership of Mindaugas, the Grand Duchy of Lithuania was established in the 1230s. Mindaugas, who later converted to Christianity, became the first and only King of Lithuania.

Throughout the following centuries, Lithuania expanded its territory through military conquests, forming alliances, and strategic marriages. It entered into a personal union with Poland through the Union of Krewo in 1386, setting the stage for the subsequent development of the Polish-Lithuanian Commonwealth, one of Europe's most significant and influential states.

The early history of Lithuania is a testament to the resilience and adaptability of its people. It reflects the gradual evolution from a collection of tribal societies to the formation of a cohesive and powerful state. This historical foundation would shape Lithuania's identity, culture, and destiny in the centuries to come.

Medieval Lithuania: Rise of the Grand Duchy

Medieval Lithuania marked a pivotal era in the nation's history, as it witnessed the rise of the Grand Duchy of Lithuania to prominence in Eastern Europe. This period, spanning from the late 12th century to the late 14th century, was characterized by territorial expansion, political consolidation, and the forging of a distinct Lithuanian identity.

The late 12th and early 13th centuries were marked by a series of struggles and conflicts as Lithuanian leaders sought to solidify their authority and expand their domains. One of the central figures in this era was Mindaugas, who is often regarded as the first and only King of Lithuania. Mindaugas ruled during a turbulent time when Lithuania was threatened by external forces, including the Teutonic Knights and the Kingdom of Poland.

Mindaugas' reign witnessed a significant development: his conversion to Christianity in an effort to gain support from Christian Europe. This marked a turning point in Lithuania's history, as it brought the nation into closer contact with Western European states. However, Mindaugas' rule was short-lived, and he faced opposition from pagan nobility. After his assassination in 1263, Lithuania returned to paganism for a period. It was during the 13th century that Lithuania began to actively resist the encroachments of the Teutonic Knights, who sought to convert the Baltic pagans and expand their territory. The Lithuanian tribes, under the leadership of leaders like

Traidenis and Vytenis, successfully defended their lands against these incursions. This period also saw the consolidation of the Lithuanian state, as various tribal regions and chieftains began to unite under a common banner. The pivotal moment came with the reign of Gediminas, who ruled from 1316 to 1341. Gediminas is often credited with expanding the Grand Duchy of Lithuania's territory significantly. He established Vilnius as the capital and worked to strengthen the duchy's position both politically and diplomatically. Gediminas' reign marked a period of relative stability, and he maintained strategic alliances with neighboring states while also actively pursuing territorial acquisitions.

One of Gediminas' most important achievements was his efforts to promote cultural exchange and religious tolerance within the Grand Duchy of Lithuania. This approach attracted various ethnic groups, including Jews and Ruthenians, to settle in the region, contributing to its cultural diversity. Under Gediminas and his successors, the Grand Duchy continued to grow and expand its influence, eventually encompassing a vast territory that stretched from the Baltic Sea in the west to the Black Sea in the south. This expansion set the stage for the future development of the Polish-Lithuanian Commonwealth, a union that would shape the course of Eastern European history for centuries to come.

Medieval Lithuania, with its territorial growth, political maneuvering, and cultural exchange, laid the foundations for the powerful and culturally diverse nation that Lithuania would become in the following centuries. It was a time of dynamic change and growth, marking an essential chapter in the nation's history.

Lithuania's Union with Poland

Lithuania's union with Poland marked a significant chapter in its history, a complex and enduring alliance that would shape the nation's destiny for centuries. This union, often referred to as the Polish-Lithuanian Commonwealth, emerged during the late medieval period and would have a profound impact on the political, cultural, and social fabric of both nations.

The roots of this union can be traced back to the late 14th century when the Lithuanian Grand Duke Jogaila, also known as Władysław II Jagiełło, entered into a personal union with the Kingdom of Poland through the Union of Krewo in 1386. This historic agreement had far-reaching consequences, as it not only united two distinct realms but also set the stage for their mutual cooperation and integration.

One of the pivotal aspects of this union was Jogaila's conversion to Christianity, a move that aligned Lithuania more closely with Western Europe and facilitated its acceptance by the Christian states of the time. This religious transformation played a significant role in forging ties with Poland, a predominantly Catholic nation.

The Polish-Lithuanian Commonwealth, formally established by the Union of Lublin in 1569, brought about a unique form of government known as a "noble republic." The state was characterized by a parliamentary system and a strong nobility that held significant power. This union allowed Lithuania to maintain its distinct identity and autonomy within the broader framework of the Commonwealth.

Under this union, Lithuania expanded its territories even further, reaching its zenith in the 17th century. At its height, the Polish-Lithuanian Commonwealth was one of the largest and most influential states in Europe, spanning from the Baltic Sea to the Black Sea.

This era witnessed a flourishing of culture and intellectual pursuits, with the Commonwealth becoming a hub for art, literature, and academia. The city of Vilnius, in particular, emerged as a vibrant center of learning and culture, attracting scholars, artists, and writers from across Europe.

However, the union was not without its challenges. Internal conflicts and external pressures, including invasions from neighboring powers such as Russia and Sweden, tested the strength of the Commonwealth. Over time, the balance of power within the union shifted, and Poland increasingly dominated the political landscape.

By the late 18th century, the Polish-Lithuanian Commonwealth faced a series of partitions by its neighboring powers, leading to the eventual dissolution of the union. In 1795, the territory of Lithuania was divided among Russia, Prussia, and Austria, erasing the political entity that had endured for centuries.

The union between Lithuania and Poland left a lasting legacy. It influenced the development of both nations' cultures, languages, and traditions. Lithuania, for example, retained a strong sense of identity, even during the union, and its language, Lithuanian, persisted as a vital aspect of its heritage.

The Lithuanian Renaissance

The Lithuanian Renaissance stands as a remarkable period in the nation's history, a time of cultural blossoming and intellectual awakening that left an indelible mark on Lithuania's identity. This era, which unfolded during the late 19th and early 20th centuries, was a pivotal chapter in Lithuania's journey to regain its independence and promote its unique cultural heritage.

At the heart of the Lithuanian Renaissance was a resurgence of national consciousness and a fervent desire to preserve and celebrate Lithuania's rich history, language, and traditions. The Lithuanian people, who had endured centuries of foreign rule and cultural suppression, embarked on a quest to rekindle their national identity.

One of the key figures of this period was Jonas Basanavičius, often regarded as the patriarch of the Lithuanian National Revival. Basanavičius, a physician, and scholar, played a pivotal role in promoting Lithuanian culture, history, and language. He founded cultural societies, published important works on Lithuanian folklore and history, and organized the Great Seimas of Vilnius in 1905, a historic assembly that laid the foundation for the Lithuanian national movement.

The Lithuanian press also played a crucial role in the Renaissance. Numerous Lithuanian-language publications, including newspapers, magazines, and books, emerged during this time. These publications not only served as a means of disseminating information but also as a vehicle for expressing national identity and fostering a sense of unity among Lithuanians.

Education was another cornerstone of the Lithuanian Renaissance. Efforts were made to establish Lithuanian-language schools and promote literacy among the population. The creation of a standardized Lithuanian alphabet and grammar system further solidified the development of the language.

The cultural revival extended to the arts, with the emergence of a vibrant literary and artistic scene. Renowned authors like Vincas Krėvė-Mickevičius and Jonas Aistis contributed to the literary landscape with their works celebrating Lithuanian folklore and history. In the world of art, painters like Mikalojus Konstantinas Čiurlionis gained recognition for their unique and expressive creations.

Music also flourished during this period, with composers like Juozas Naujalis and Česlovas Sasnauskas composing patriotic and folk-inspired compositions that resonated deeply with the Lithuanian people.

The Lithuanian Renaissance was not without its challenges. The era was marked by political turmoil, as Lithuania sought to assert its independence from foreign rule, particularly from the Russian Empire. The First World War and the subsequent collapse of empires in Europe provided a window of opportunity for Lithuania to declare its independence, which it did on February 16, 1918.

The Lithuanian Renaissance, with its cultural revival, political awakening, and tireless efforts to preserve the nation's heritage, remains a testament to the resilience of the Lithuanian people. It laid the groundwork for Lithuania's modern identity as a sovereign nation, embracing its language, culture, and history with pride. This transformative period continues to be celebrated and remembered as a vital chapter in Lithuania's history.

Lithuania in the Russian Empire

Lithuania's history within the Russian Empire is a complex narrative that unfolds against the backdrop of a vast and powerful empire. This period, spanning from the late 18th century to the early 20th century, was characterized by significant political, social, and cultural transformations that profoundly impacted the Lithuanian people.

The late 18th century marked a turning point for Lithuania when it became part of the Russian Empire following the partitions of the Polish-Lithuanian Commonwealth. The region had previously been part of the Polish-Lithuanian Commonwealth, a union that had allowed Lithuania to maintain a degree of autonomy within a larger political entity.

Under Russian rule, Lithuania experienced a series of changes that affected nearly every aspect of life. The Russian Empire was known for its centralization of power, and this centralization extended to the regions it controlled, including Lithuania. The Lithuanian nobility, which had historically held considerable influence in the Grand Duchy of Lithuania, saw its power diminished under Russian administration.

The Russian government imposed various policies aimed at Russification, which included efforts to promote the Russian language and Orthodox Christianity. Lithuanian culture and language faced suppression, with restrictions on the use of the Lithuanian language in education and publications. Despite these challenges, Lithuanians persevered in preserving their cultural heritage through underground publications and cultural activities. Economic changes also marked Lithuania's time within the Russian Empire. The region became more integrated into the Russian economy, with the development of infrastructure such as railways and the growth of industries. This economic shift had both positive and negative consequences for the Lithuanian population, as it brought industrialization but also led to urbanization and changes in traditional rural life.

Lithuania's relationship with the Russian Empire was marked by moments of resistance and political activism. In the late 19th and early 20th centuries, Lithuania saw the emergence of various nationalist movements and political parties advocating for greater autonomy or even independence from Russia. These movements played a pivotal role in shaping Lithuania's political future.

The early 20th century brought significant changes to the Russian Empire, including the turmoil of the First World War and the Russian Revolution of 1917. These events created opportunities for Lithuania to assert its independence. On February 16, 1918, Lithuania declared its sovereignty, marking the end of its time within the Russian Empire and the beginning of a new era as a modern European nation.

The period of Lithuania in the Russian Empire was marked by a complex interplay of political control, cultural suppression, economic transformation, and resistance. It tested the resilience of the Lithuanian people and laid the groundwork for the nation's subsequent struggle for independence. Lithuania's history within the Russian Empire remains a crucial chapter in its journey toward sovereignty and self-determination.

Independence and the Interwar Period

Independence and the Interwar Period in Lithuania represent a critical juncture in the nation's history, a time of newfound sovereignty and the challenges of nation-building in the aftermath of World War I. This era, which spans from the end of World War I in 1918 to the onset of World War II in 1939, was marked by Lithuania's emergence as a modern European nation-state.

The end of World War I brought about a seismic shift in the geopolitical landscape of Eastern Europe. Lithuania, along with its Baltic neighbors Latvia and Estonia, seized the opportunity to declare independence from the crumbling Russian Empire and the defeated German Empire. On February 16, 1918, Lithuania proclaimed its independence, reasserting its status as a sovereign nation after centuries of foreign rule.

The newly established Lithuanian state faced numerous challenges as it sought to consolidate its independence and assert its territorial integrity. The aftermath of World War I was a period of political instability in the region, and Lithuania had to contend with various threats to its sovereignty, including territorial disputes and military conflicts.

One of the defining moments of this era was the Lithuanian-Polish War of 1919-1920, a conflict over disputed border territories. This war, which had far-reaching consequences for both nations, ultimately ended with the signing of the Suwałki Agreement in 1920, settling some of the border issues between Lithuania and Poland.

The Interwar Period in Lithuania was marked by efforts to establish a stable government and build the foundations of a modern state. The country adopted a democratic parliamentary system, with a constitution adopted in 1922 that established Lithuania as a democratic republic. It also laid the groundwork for a legal system and institutions that would govern the nation.

Economically, Lithuania faced the challenges of reconstruction and development. The agrarian sector was a significant component of the economy, and land reform aimed to redistribute land to peasants. Additionally, industrialization and economic modernization efforts were underway.

Culturally, the Interwar Period was a time of national revival and expression. The Lithuanian language was promoted, and efforts were made to strengthen cultural institutions, education, and the arts. This period saw the emergence of significant cultural figures and literary works that celebrated Lithuanian heritage.

However, this period was not without difficulties. Lithuania faced internal political tensions, economic struggles, and external pressures from neighboring powers, including the Soviet Union. In 1926, a coup d'état led by Antanas Smetona resulted in a shift towards a more authoritarian regime, which aimed to stabilize the country but also limited political freedoms.

The Interwar Period in Lithuania was a time of nation-building, marked by achievements and challenges alike. The nation worked to establish its identity, institutions, and place in the international community. This chapter in Lithuania's history laid the groundwork for the subsequent events of World War II and the post-war era, shaping the nation's identity and resilience for generations to come.

World War II and Soviet Occupation

World War II and the subsequent Soviet occupation of Lithuania were tumultuous and deeply impactful chapters in the nation's history. These events, which unfolded from the late 1930s into the 1940s, brought unprecedented challenges and upheaval to Lithuania and its people.

The outbreak of World War II in 1939 had profound consequences for Lithuania, as the nation found itself caught in the crossfire of shifting alliances and power struggles among neighboring states. In September 1939, Nazi Germany and the Soviet Union signed the Molotov-Ribbentrop Pact, a non-aggression treaty that included a secret protocol dividing Eastern Europe into spheres of influence.

As a result of this pact, Lithuania became a target for Soviet expansion. In June 1940, Soviet forces occupied the country, and a puppet government was installed. This marked the beginning of a period of Sovietization, where Lithuania was subjected to Soviet policies and control.

The Soviet occupation had a profound impact on all aspects of life in Lithuania. Political repression, censorship, and suppression of dissent became common. Private property was nationalized, and collective farms were established, leading to significant changes in the agricultural sector.

One of the most tragic aspects of this period was the mass deportations and executions carried out by the Soviet authorities. Thousands of Lithuanians, including intellectuals, politicians, and ordinary citizens, were arrested, deported to Siberia, or executed. These actions aimed to suppress any resistance and maintain control over the population.

The situation took a dramatic turn with the onset of Operation Barbarossa in June 1941 when Nazi Germany invaded the Soviet Union. Lithuanians, in some cases, initially welcomed the German forces as liberators from Soviet oppression. However, this hope was short-lived, as the Nazis soon imposed their own brutal occupation regime.

During the Nazi occupation, Lithuania's Jewish population suffered horrific atrocities, with mass killings and the establishment of concentration camps in the country. It is estimated that tens of thousands of Lithuanian Jews were murdered during this period.

As World War II drew to a close, the Soviet Union once again reasserted control over Lithuania. In 1944-1945, the Red Army reoccupied the country, leading to another wave of repression, deportations, and the suppression of political and cultural life.

Lithuania remained under Soviet control for the next several decades, enduring the hardships and limitations of a communist regime. The struggle for independence, however, continued to simmer beneath the surface, culminating in the late 1980s with the Singing Revolution, a series of mass protests and demonstrations that paved the way for Lithuania's reassertion of sovereignty and independence in 1990.

The Baltic Way: Freedom Regained

In the late 1980s, the Baltic States, including Lithuania, found themselves at the forefront of a remarkable and peaceful movement for freedom known as the Baltic Way. This extraordinary event, which took place on August 23, 1989, was a demonstration of unity, determination, and the unwavering desire for independence that had been suppressed for decades under Soviet rule.

The Baltic Way was a human chain that spanned approximately 600 kilometers (370 miles) across the three Baltic States: Lithuania, Latvia, and Estonia. It was a profound display of solidarity and a symbolic act that sent a powerful message to the world. Participants, numbering in the hundreds of thousands, linked hands to form an unbroken chain that traversed the entire length of the Baltic States, from the capital cities of Vilnius, Riga, and Tallinn to the countryside and small towns.

This peaceful protest was organized to commemorate the 50th anniversary of the Molotov-Ribbentrop Pact, the secret agreement between Nazi Germany and the Soviet Union that had led to the occupation of the Baltic States in 1940. It was a solemn reminder of the suffering and oppression that the Baltic nations had endured under both Nazi and Soviet regimes.

The Baltic Way was not merely a symbolic gesture; it was a call for freedom and a demand for recognition of the Baltic States' right to self-determination. Participants carried national flags, sang patriotic songs, and expressed their unwavering commitment to regaining their independence.

The international community watched in awe as the human chain stretched across the Baltic States, capturing the world's attention and garnering support for the Baltic cause. It was a testament to the peaceful and determined spirit of the Baltic people, who yearned for the restoration of their sovereignty and the right to govern themselves.

The impact of the Baltic Way extended far beyond the event itself. It galvanized the Baltic States' quest for independence and spurred diplomatic efforts to achieve international recognition. The solidarity displayed on that fateful day inspired similar movements in other Soviet-occupied nations and contributed to the eventual dissolution of the Soviet Union itself.

In the years that followed the Baltic Way, Lithuania and its Baltic neighbors continued their struggle for independence. On March 11, 1990, Lithuania became the first Soviet republic to declare its sovereignty, and it later declared full independence on March 11, 1990. Estonia and Latvia followed suit, and by the end of 1991, all three Baltic States had regained their independence.

The Baltic Way remains a cherished and iconic moment in the history of Lithuania and the Baltic States. It serves as a testament to the power of unity, peaceful protest, and the enduring spirit of those who yearn for freedom. The chains of oppression were broken, and the Baltic States emerged as sovereign nations, once again able to determine their own destinies.

Modern Lithuania: A European Nation

Modern Lithuania stands as a vibrant and resilient European nation, a testament to the enduring spirit of its people and their commitment to democracy, freedom, and prosperity. Since regaining independence in the early 1990s, Lithuania has undergone remarkable transformations on multiple fronts, solidifying its position as a dynamic member of the European family.

One of the defining moments in Lithuania's modern history was its declaration of independence from the Soviet Union on March 11, 1990, and subsequent restoration of full sovereignty in September 1991. This momentous achievement marked the culmination of decades of resistance, symbolized by events like the Baltic Way, and the unwavering determination to chart a new course as a free nation.

The early years of independence were marked by significant challenges, including economic transitions, the reestablishment of democratic institutions, and the reintegration of society into the global community. Lithuania embraced market reforms, privatized state-owned enterprises, and embarked on a path of economic liberalization that led to impressive growth and prosperity in the subsequent decades.

In 2004, Lithuania achieved another milestone by joining the European Union (EU) and NATO, solidifying its place within the Western democratic community. EU membership brought access to a single market, financial assistance for development, and the opportunity to participate in shaping European policies and values.

Lithuania has actively contributed to European cooperation, taking its role seriously in various EU institutions and initiatives. The country has embraced the euro as its currency, further integrating its economy into the European financial system.

In the realm of security, Lithuania, like its Baltic neighbors, has been a staunch supporter of NATO's collective defense efforts, recognizing the importance of a strong transatlantic alliance in safeguarding regional stability and security. It has also demonstrated a commitment to defense spending and modernization to enhance its security posture.

Lithuania's modern landscape is characterized by a thriving economy, a robust educational system, and a vibrant cultural scene. The capital city, Vilnius, is a dynamic hub of business and culture, with a rich historical heritage that includes a beautifully preserved Old Town designated as a UNESCO World Heritage site.

The Lithuanian people have embraced their role as active European citizens, participating in democratic processes, civil society activities, and cultural exchanges. The country has made significant strides in preserving its cultural heritage, fostering the arts, and promoting the Lithuanian language.

Lithuania's journey in the 21st century has been marked by resilience, adaptability, and an unwavering commitment to European values. It is a nation that has redefined itself as a European democracy, forging strong ties with its neighbors and contributing to the broader European project.

Lithuanian Wildlife: A Natural Wonderland

Lithuania, often celebrated for its rich history and vibrant culture, is also home to a stunning array of wildlife and natural wonders. Nestled in the northeastern part of Europe, this Baltic nation boasts diverse ecosystems, from dense forests to pristine wetlands and a picturesque coastline along the Baltic Sea. The country's commitment to conservation has helped protect its unique biodiversity, making Lithuania a true natural wonderland.

Forests are an integral part of Lithuania's landscape, covering approximately one-third of its territory. These woodlands are a haven for a variety of wildlife species, including the iconic European bison, the continent's heaviest land animal. Lithuania plays a vital role in bison conservation efforts, with several herds thriving in protected areas.

Lithuania's lush forests are also home to an array of mammals, such as deer, wild boar, foxes, and European beavers. The pristine woodlands offer ample foraging grounds and shelter for these creatures, making it a perfect habitat for observing their natural behaviors.

Wetlands are another remarkable feature of Lithuania's natural landscape. The country's many lakes, rivers, and marshes create ideal conditions for waterfowl and other wetland species. In fact, Lithuania is a crucial stopover point for migratory birds, with countless flocks passing through during their seasonal journeys.

One of the most renowned wetland areas in Lithuania is the Nemunas Delta, where the Nemunas River flows into the Baltic Sea. This region teems with birdlife, including various species of herons, swans, and ducks. Birdwatchers flock to the delta to witness the mesmerizing spectacle of thousands of birds in their natural habitat.

The Baltic Sea coastline, stretching over 90 kilometers (56 miles), is another vital ecosystem in Lithuania. It harbors diverse marine life, from fish and seals to seabirds. The Curonian Spit, a UNESCO World Heritage site shared with Russia, is a unique sand dune peninsula that shelters rare plant species and provides a habitat for migratory birds.

Lithuania's commitment to nature conservation is evident in its network of protected areas, including national parks, nature reserves, and wildlife sanctuaries. These areas safeguard the country's biodiversity and provide opportunities for ecotourism, allowing visitors to connect with the natural world while respecting its fragility.

In the underwater realm, Lithuania's numerous lakes are home to a variety of fish species, including perch, pike, and roach. Anglers from all over the world are drawn to the country's serene lakes and rivers for a chance to catch these prized fish.

Lithuania's rich natural heritage extends to its flora as well. The country's meadows burst with colorful wildflowers during the summer months, creating a vibrant tapestry of nature. Rare and protected plant species, such as the lady's slipper orchid, can be found in Lithuania's pristine meadows and forests.

The Flora and Fauna of Lithuania

Lithuania, a land of diverse landscapes and ecosystems, is blessed with a rich tapestry of flora and fauna that thrives within its borders. From pristine forests and meadows to wetlands and coastline, this Baltic nation boasts a remarkable array of natural life, making it a haven for both wildlife enthusiasts and nature lovers.

Forests, covering roughly a third of Lithuania's land, are a defining feature of its natural environment. Within these woodlands, you'll encounter a fascinating mix of tree species, including pine, spruce, oak, birch, and beech. These forests serve as the home to an impressive range of wildlife.

One of Lithuania's most emblematic and conservation-worthy species is the European bison, often referred to as the wisent. These massive creatures, Europe's heaviest land animals, roam protected areas of Lithuania's forests. Dedicated conservation efforts have helped the bison population rebound, making Lithuania an essential player in the wisent's preservation.

Beyond the bison, Lithuania's forests are home to an array of mammals, both large and small. Herds of deer and wild boar traverse the woodlands, while foxes, martens, and European hares navigate the underbrush. The European beaver, once nearly extinct in Lithuania, has made a remarkable comeback due to successful reintroduction programs.

Wetlands are another prominent feature of Lithuania's natural landscape. Numerous lakes, rivers, and marshes create ideal habitats for waterfowl and amphibians. During the migration seasons, Lithuania becomes a vital stopover for countless birds, with wetlands teeming with swans, ducks, and herons.

The Nemunas Delta, where the Nemunas River meets the Baltic Sea, stands out as a significant wetland region and a haven for birdwatchers. Countless bird species, from elegant swans to graceful storks, find refuge in this unique environment.

Lithuania's 90-kilometer (56-mile) Baltic Sea coastline harbors its own special ecosystem. The Curonian Spit, a UNESCO World Heritage site, is a sandy peninsula shared with Russia. This remarkable landform shelters an array of plant life and provides a critical habitat for migratory birds and seals.

In the underwater realm, Lithuania's lakes hold various fish species, including perch, pike, and roach. Anglers flock to these serene waters to test their skills and enjoy the tranquility of the landscape.

The country's flora is equally captivating. Meadows, particularly during the summer months, burst into a vibrant display of wildflowers, coloring the countryside with hues of purple, yellow, and red. Rare and protected plant species, like the lady's slipper orchid, can be found throughout Lithuania's meadows and forests.

Lithuania's commitment to nature conservation is evident through its network of protected areas, including national parks, nature reserves, and wildlife sanctuaries. These areas play a crucial role in safeguarding the nation's biodiversity while providing opportunities for ecotourism and educational experiences.

In conclusion, Lithuania's remarkable flora and fauna are woven into the fabric of its identity as a nation. The country's dedication to preserving its natural heritage has ensured that it remains a sanctuary for diverse wildlife and plant life. Whether you're exploring the pristine forests, wandering through wildflower-strewn meadows, or observing migratory birds, Lithuania's natural world offers an ever-evolving tapestry of beauty and biodiversity.

Baltic Delights: Lithuanian Cuisine

Lithuanian cuisine, deeply rooted in the nation's agricultural traditions and culinary heritage, offers a delightful journey through flavors that reflect the country's history and geography. From hearty, comforting dishes to sweet treats and unique culinary traditions, Lithuanian food is a reflection of the nation's culture and the resilience of its people.

Potatoes, often referred to as "the second bread," play a central role in Lithuanian cuisine. These versatile tubers find their way into a variety of dishes, from the beloved potato pancakes known as "bulviniai blynai" to hearty potato dumplings called "cepelinai." Cepelinai, often stuffed with meat, curd cheese, or mushrooms, are a symbol of Lithuanian comfort food.

Another staple in Lithuanian cooking is rye bread. Dark and dense, Lithuanian rye bread is renowned for its robust flavor. It's served as a side to many dishes or used as a base for open-faced sandwiches called "sumustiniai." These sandwiches often feature an array of toppings, including smoked fish, cheese, and vegetables.

Lithuanian cuisine also has a strong connection to dairy products. Curd cheese, known as "varškė," is a favorite ingredient, used in both savory and sweet dishes. A classic Lithuanian dessert is "varškės sūreliai," small curd cheese dumplings served with sour cream and sugar.

Meat plays a significant role in Lithuanian cuisine, with pork being the most popular choice. Sausages, such as "dešra" and "šaltiena" (jellied pig's feet), are common delicacies. The preparation of meat often involves smoking or curing, adding depth and complexity to the flavors.

Mushrooms are another beloved ingredient in Lithuanian cooking, with the country's forests providing an abundant supply. Various mushroom dishes, including mushroom soup and mushroom-stuffed pastries, are enjoyed throughout the year.

Fish, particularly freshwater fish like pike and perch, are abundant in Lithuania's numerous lakes and rivers. Smoked or marinated fish, such as "šalčiai" (pickled herring), are cherished components of the cuisine, often served with potatoes or rye bread.

Lithuanian celebrations and festivals offer a glimpse into the nation's culinary traditions. The "Kūčios" Christmas Eve feast is a cherished tradition, featuring an array of meatless dishes, including twelve different dishes representing the twelve apostles. Another significant event is "Joninės" or St. John's Eve, celebrated with bonfires and the ritualistic preparation of "Žirniai su spirgučiais," a dish made of peas and bacon.

To satisfy a sweet tooth, Lithuanian desserts and pastries abound. "Šakotis" is a distinctive tree-shaped cake, often served at weddings and special occasions. Honey cakes, fruit-filled pastries, and "bandelės" (sweet rolls) are among the many sweet treats that grace Lithuanian tables.

Lithuanian beverages include "gira," a homemade fermented bread drink, and "midus," a traditional honey mead. Both beverages are deeply ingrained in Lithuanian culture and are often enjoyed during festive gatherings.

Lithuanian cuisine is a celebration of tradition and a testament to the country's enduring spirit. It reflects the deep connection between the people and their land, where the bounty of forests, fields, and waters provides the ingredients for a culinary heritage that continues to be savored and cherished. Whether savoring the comforting flavors of a potato dish, indulging in a sweet pastry, or raising a toast with a traditional beverage, Lithuanian cuisine offers a delightful exploration of the nation's rich and flavorful culture.

Traditional Lithuanian Dishes

Traditional Lithuanian dishes are a delightful journey into the heart of this Baltic nation's culinary heritage. These recipes have been lovingly passed down through generations, reflecting the country's history, culture, and agricultural traditions. Let's explore some of the iconic dishes that have graced Lithuanian tables for centuries.

Cepelinai: Often considered the king of Lithuanian cuisine, cepelinai are large potato dumplings stuffed with various fillings. The most common fillings include minced meat, curd cheese, and mushrooms. They are named after their resemblance to zeppelins, the famous airships.

Kugelis: Kugelis is a beloved Lithuanian potato pudding. Grated potatoes are mixed with eggs, onions, and sometimes bacon before being baked to a golden brown. It's a hearty and comforting dish, often enjoyed with sour cream.

Bulviniai blynai: Lithuanian potato pancakes, or bulviniai blynai, are a staple in Lithuanian homes. Grated potatoes are mixed with flour, eggs, and spices, then fried to crispy perfection. They are typically served with sour cream or applesauce.

Šaltibarščiai: This vibrant and refreshing beet soup, often called cold borscht, is a staple in Lithuanian summer menus. It features beets, cucumbers, buttermilk, and dill, creating a bright pink soup with a tangy flavor.

Koldūnai: Koldūnai are small, delicate dumplings, similar to pierogi. They are typically filled with minced meat, mushrooms, or curd cheese and served with sour cream. They make a popular appetizer or main course.

Balandėliai: Balandėliai, or cabbage rolls, are made by wrapping minced meat and rice in cabbage leaves. They are simmered in a flavorful tomato sauce until tender and served with sour cream.

Kugel: Kugel is a sweet or savory baked pudding made from noodles, potatoes, or bread. Sweet kugel often includes raisins, sugar, and cinnamon, while savory versions may have vegetables and spices.

Silkė su morkomis: Herring with carrots is a traditional Lithuanian dish enjoyed during celebrations and holidays. The herring is typically marinated in a sweet and sour sauce and served with carrots.

Kisielius: This fruit soup is a popular Lithuanian dessert. It's made by simmering various berries with sugar and starch until it thickens. Kisielius is served cold and enjoyed as a refreshing summer treat.

Rugelach: Rugelach are small pastries filled with jam, nuts, and spices. They have Jewish origins but have become a beloved dessert in Lithuania, especially during the holiday season.

Rugpjūčio pirsteliai: Translating to "August Fingers," these are sweet, twisted pastries often enjoyed during the harvest season. They are made with a yeast dough and sprinkled with sugar.

Lithuanian cuisine embodies the country's connection to the land and its history of farming and agriculture. These traditional dishes, often made with simple ingredients, carry the flavors and memories of generations past. Whether it's the comforting aroma of kugelis, the crispy texture of bulviniai blynai, or the sweet satisfaction of rugelach, Lithuanian cuisine is a celebration of heritage and a testament to the enduring culinary traditions of this Baltic nation.

Lithuanian Beverages: Beer, Mead, and More

Lithuania, like many European nations, has a rich tradition of brewing and distilling beverages that reflect its history and cultural heritage. From beer to mead and a variety of unique concoctions, the country's drink offerings are as diverse as its landscapes.

Beer: Beer holds a special place in Lithuanian culture. It's not just a beverage; it's a symbol of camaraderie and celebration. Lithuanians have been brewing beer for centuries, with a history dating back to medieval times. The country's beer culture is so deeply rooted that it's often said that every Lithuanian village has its brewery. Lithuanian beer is typically light, crisp, and refreshing, making it a popular choice, especially during the warm summer months. The most famous Lithuanian beer is "Švyturys," which has a history dating back to 1784. Varieties like "Švyturys Ekstra" and "Švyturys Baltijos" are enjoyed nationwide.

Mead: Mead, known as "midus" in Lithuanian, is a traditional honey-based alcoholic beverage with a long history in the region. It's often associated with special occasions, including weddings and festivals. Lithuanian mead is typically made with honey, water, and various herbs and spices, which can impart a range of flavors, from sweet and floral to spicy and aromatic. It's a drink that invokes a sense of tradition and celebration.

Gira: Gira is a fermented beverage made from black or rye bread, sugar, and yeast. It's mildly alcoholic and has a taste that's somewhat reminiscent of root beer. Gira is a homemade specialty in Lithuania, with families often brewing their own batches. It's a refreshing drink enjoyed during the summer and can be served chilled with a slice of lemon.

Kvass: Kvass is another fermented beverage that has found its way into Lithuanian culture. It's made from bread, most commonly rye bread, and is known for its slightly sour and effervescent taste. Kvass is often sweetened with sugar and flavored with herbs and berries. It's a popular choice for quenching thirst, especially on hot days.

Žalioji Arbata: Lithuania has a strong tradition of herbal teas, and "žalioji arbata," or green tea, is a common choice. While it's not a traditional Lithuanian beverage, it has gained popularity for its health benefits and refreshing qualities. Many Lithuanians enjoy sipping green tea, often with honey or lemon.

Vodka: Vodka, like in many Eastern European countries, is a staple alcoholic beverage. Lithuania has its own brands and variations, known for their purity and quality. It's typically consumed straight and chilled, often as a toast during celebrations and gatherings.

Cider: Cider has also gained popularity in recent years, with local producers crafting their own versions using apples and other fruits. Lithuanian cider is known for its crisp and fruity flavors, making it a refreshing alternative to beer, especially in the warmer seasons.

Lithuanian beverages are a reflection of the country's deep-rooted traditions and the importance of social gatherings and celebrations. Whether it's sharing a cold beer with friends, raising a glass of mead to toast a special occasion, or sipping on a cup of herbal tea, these beverages are an integral part of Lithuanian culture, offering a taste of the country's history and hospitality.

The Sweet Side of Lithuania: Desserts and Pastries

Lithuania's culinary heritage is not limited to savory dishes; it also boasts a delectable array of desserts and pastries that offer a sweet conclusion to a traditional Lithuanian meal. These sweet treats are not just confections; they are a reflection of the country's history, culture, and love for all things sugary.

Šakotis: Often referred to as the "tree cake" due to its distinctive tree-like shape, Šakotis is an iconic Lithuanian dessert. It's made from a batter of eggs, sugar, and flour, which is slowly poured onto a rotating spit. As the layers cook and caramelize, they form a unique and visually striking cake. Šakotis is often enjoyed during special occasions and celebrations, such as weddings and birthdays.

Rugelach: Rugelach, while originally of Jewish origin, has become a beloved pastry in Lithuania. These bite-sized delights consist of dough rolled around sweet fillings like jam, nuts, and spices. They are baked to a golden brown and dusted with powdered sugar, creating a perfect balance of textures and flavors.

Kūčiukai: Kūčiukai are tiny, slightly sweetened dough balls that are traditionally made for Christmas Eve, also known as Kūčios. These small pastries are enjoyed by the handful, often dipped in poppy seed milk or honey. They represent a cherished holiday tradition that brings families together.

Spurgos: Spurgos are Lithuanian doughnuts, and they come in various shapes and sizes. These deep-fried delights are typically filled with jam or custard and dusted with powdered sugar. They are a popular choice for breakfast or as a sweet snack throughout the day.

Bandelės: Bandelės are sweet rolls, often filled with jam or curd cheese. They are a simple yet satisfying treat that pairs perfectly with a cup of tea or coffee. Bandelės can be enjoyed at any time of day and are especially popular during gatherings and celebrations.

Žagareliai: Žagareliai are Lithuanian twisted cookies that are both crunchy and tender. They are made from a simple dough of flour, butter, sugar, and eggs, twisted into intricate shapes before baking. These cookies are a delightful addition to any dessert spread.

Kisielius: While kisielius was mentioned earlier as a fruit soup, it also doubles as a sweet dessert. When served cold, this fruit soup becomes a refreshing and tangy treat that's often enjoyed during hot summer days. It's made from various berries, sugar, and starch.

Obuolių pyragas: Lithuanian apple pie, or obuolių pyragas, is a classic dessert that highlights the country's abundant apple orchards. The pie is typically made with thinly sliced apples, sugar, and cinnamon, all encased in a flaky pastry crust.

Meduoliai: Meduoliai are honey cookies with a hint of spice. These cookies are often shaped like hearts or other festive figures and are a delightful addition to holiday gatherings and celebrations.

Lithuanian desserts and pastries offer a sweet ending to any meal and a glimpse into the country's culinary traditions. From the intricate layers of Šakotis to the comforting simplicity of kūčiukai, these treats are a testament to Lithuania's love for all things sweet and a cherished part of its cultural heritage.

Must-Try Lithuanian Food Experiences

Lithuania, a hidden gem in the culinary world, offers a range of food experiences that are a delightful blend of tradition, culture, and taste. Whether you're an adventurous foodie or simply curious to explore the flavors of this Baltic nation, here are some must-try Lithuanian food experiences that will leave your taste buds tingling and your stomach satisfied.

1. Cepelinai: These hearty potato dumplings are a Lithuanian icon and a must-try for anyone visiting the country. Shaped like zeppelins, they are often stuffed with minced meat, curd cheese, or mushrooms and served with sour cream. The combination of soft potato dough and flavorful fillings is a culinary delight.

2. Kugelis: Dive into Lithuanian comfort food with kugelis, a potato pudding that's crispy on the outside and creamy on the inside. Made with grated potatoes, onions, eggs, and sometimes bacon, it's a hearty dish often enjoyed with sour cream or applesauce.

3. Cold Borscht (Šaltibarščiai): This vibrant pink soup is a refreshing summer favorite. Made with beets, cucumbers, buttermilk, and dill, it offers a delightful balance of flavors, with a touch of tanginess. It's typically served chilled and is perfect for hot Lithuanian summers.

4. Lithuanian Rye Bread: Lithuania takes its bread seriously, and you'll find a variety of rye breads that are both delicious and nutritious. Dark and dense, Lithuanian rye bread is perfect with butter, cheese, or as a base for open-faced sandwiches.

5. Herring with Carrots (Silkė su Morkomis): If you're a seafood enthusiast, don't miss out on this marinated herring dish served with carrots. It's a flavorful and slightly tangy delight, often enjoyed as an appetizer or part of a festive spread.

6. Lithuanian Beer: Lithuania's beer culture is deeply ingrained in its social fabric. Try a glass of Lithuanian beer, often light, crisp, and perfect for quenching your thirst on a warm summer day. Local favorites like "Švyturys" offer a taste of the country's brewing traditions.

7. Lithuanian Mead (Midus): For a taste of history, savor Lithuanian mead. Made from honey, water, and a blend of herbs and spices, mead is both sweet and aromatic. It's often associated with special occasions and has a unique flavor profile.

8. Kūčiukai: These tiny dough balls are a Christmas tradition in Lithuania. Served during the festive Kūčios dinner, they are sweet and slightly crunchy, often dipped in poppy seed milk or honey.

9. Lithuanian Pastries: Delight in Lithuanian pastries like rugelach, small rolled pastries filled with jam and nuts, and spurgos, Lithuanian doughnuts filled with various sweet fillings.

10. Exploring Local Markets: To truly immerse yourself in Lithuanian food culture, visit local markets like the Vilnius Central Market or Kaunas Farmers' Market. Here, you can sample fresh local produce, artisanal cheeses, and an array of traditional Lithuanian dishes.

Lithuania's culinary scene offers a taste of the country's rich history and agricultural heritage. Whether you're savoring the flavors of cepelinai, enjoying a bowl of cold borscht on a warm day, or raising a glass of Lithuanian beer, each culinary experience is an invitation to explore the unique and delicious world of Lithuanian cuisine.

Vilnius: Lithuania's Capital and Heart

Nestled in the heart of the Baltic region lies Vilnius, the capital of Lithuania and a city that embodies the nation's rich history, vibrant culture, and enduring spirit. As you explore this enchanting city, you'll discover a place where the past seamlessly intertwines with the present, creating a tapestry of experiences that captivate the senses and leave an indelible mark on your soul.

A City of History: Vilnius is a city steeped in history, with roots dating back to the early Middle Ages. Its Old Town, a UNESCO World Heritage site, is a living testament to the city's enduring heritage. Stroll through narrow cobblestone streets and you'll encounter architectural treasures spanning centuries, from Gothic cathedrals to Baroque churches and charming Renaissance-era townhouses. The iconic Gediminas' Tower, perched atop a hill, offers panoramic views of the city and a glimpse into its medieval past.

Cultural Crossroads: Vilnius has long been a melting pot of cultures, a place where East meets West. Its rich tapestry of influences is reflected in its diverse architecture, traditions, and cuisine. The city's architectural ensemble is a testament to this cultural crossroads, with Orthodox churches standing next to Catholic cathedrals and synagogues. Vilnius has a rich Jewish heritage, once earning it the nickname "Jerusalem of the North."

A Hub of Learning: Vilnius is home to one of Europe's oldest universities, Vilnius University, founded in 1579. The institution has played a pivotal role in the city's intellectual and cultural life. Its historic campus, adorned with courtyards and frescoed ceilings, is a testament to the pursuit of knowledge that has thrived here for centuries.

A City of Green Spaces: Despite its rich history and urban vibrancy, Vilnius is a city that embraces nature. Numerous parks and green spaces, including Vingis Park and Belmontas Park, provide a respite from the hustle and bustle of city life. The Neris River, meandering through the city, offers scenic walks and opportunities for relaxation.

A Modern Metropolis: While Vilnius celebrates its history, it also embraces modernity. The city has a thriving arts scene, with numerous galleries and cultural events. Its dining scene showcases Lithuanian cuisine alongside international flavors. Modern skyscrapers stand in harmony with historic facades, creating a cityscape that reflects Vilnius's dynamic spirit.

A Place of Festivals: Vilnius is a city that loves to celebrate. Throughout the year, it hosts a multitude of festivals that showcase music, arts, and culture. The Vilnius International Film Festival, Užgavėnės (Shrove Tuesday), and the Vilnius Jazz Festival are just a few examples of the vibrant cultural scene.

Warm Hospitality: Lithuanians are known for their warm and welcoming nature, and this hospitality is palpable in Vilnius. Whether you're savoring traditional Lithuanian dishes in a cozy restaurant or striking up a conversation with locals in a cafe, you'll feel the genuine friendliness of the people.

Intriguing Stories: Vilnius is a city of stories, with tales of grand dukes, poets, revolutionaries, and artists echoing through its streets. It's a place where history comes alive, inviting you to uncover its secrets and mysteries.

As you explore Vilnius, you'll find that it's not just a city; it's a living canvas of history and culture. It's a place where past and present converge, where traditions are honored, and where the spirit of Lithuania thrives. Vilnius is a city that captures the heart and soul, inviting you to become part of its story.

Kaunas: The Historical City of Culture

Nestled along the banks of the confluence of the Nemunas and Neris rivers, Kaunas stands as a testament to Lithuania's rich history and cultural heritage. This historical city, the country's second-largest, is a tapestry of stories, a place where past and present intersect in a harmonious blend of tradition and modernity.

With a history dating back to the 11th century, Kaunas has witnessed the rise and fall of empires, the ebb and flow of artistic movements, and the enduring spirit of its people. As you explore this city, you'll find yourself immersed in a world of captivating narratives and captivating architecture.

The heart of Kaunas is its Old Town, a labyrinth of cobblestone streets lined with centuries-old buildings. The Town Hall, a magnificent Gothic structure dating back to the 16th century, is a focal point, where markets and festivities have unfolded for generations.

One cannot speak of Kaunas without mentioning its vibrant cultural scene. The city is a hub for artistic expression, with numerous galleries, theaters, and cultural events taking place year-round. The M. K. Čiurlionis National Art Museum, named after Lithuania's famed painter and composer, showcases a stunning collection of his works.

Kaunas is also home to Vytautas Magnus University, a prestigious institution that has been at the forefront of Lithuanian education for nearly a century. Its historic campus, adorned with grand facades and lush gardens, is a testament to the pursuit of knowledge that thrives within its walls.

Venturing beyond the Old Town, you'll discover the green lungs of Kaunas. Žaliakalnis, a picturesque neighborhood, is crowned by the Aleksotas Funicular Railway, which offers breathtaking views of the city. The Pazaislis Monastery, a serene Baroque masterpiece, is a tranquil retreat on the shores of Lake Kaunas.

Kaunas also boasts a thriving culinary scene, where traditional Lithuanian dishes are celebrated alongside international flavors. Cafes and restaurants dot the cityscape, offering a taste of both local and global cuisine.

Throughout the year, Kaunas hosts a multitude of festivals that showcase music, arts, and culture. The Kaunas Jazz Festival, Devilstone, and the International Kaunas Film Festival are just a few examples of the vibrant cultural tapestry that envelops the city.

Beyond its cultural riches, Kaunas is a city of warm hospitality. The people of Kaunas are known for their friendliness and genuine warmth, making visitors feel right at home.

As you traverse the streets of Kaunas, you'll find that it's more than just a city; it's a living canvas of history and culture. It's a place where stories unfold with each step, where the echoes of the past resonate alongside the rhythms of the present. Kaunas is a city that invites you to immerse yourself in its tapestry, to explore its historical wonders, and to experience the warmth of its people.

Klaipėda: Lithuania's Seaport Gem

On the western edge of Lithuania, where the Curonian Lagoon meets the Baltic Sea, lies the coastal city of Klaipėda. This vibrant seaport gem holds a unique place in Lithuania's cultural and historical landscape. As you step onto its shores, you'll discover a city that harmonizes the maritime spirit with a rich tapestry of traditions and an unmistakable coastal charm.

Klaipėda boasts a history that spans centuries, with its roots tracing back to the medieval era. The city's Old Town, characterized by its narrow cobblestone streets and colorful buildings, whispers tales of Hanseatic merchants and the Teutonic Knights who once walked these same paths. The iconic Theatre Square, framed by elegant architecture, serves as a central hub for cultural events and gatherings.

One of Klaipėda's most distinctive features is the Curonian Spit, a UNESCO World Heritage site that stretches across the lagoon. This unique landform, characterized by shifting sand dunes, pine forests, and serene beaches, is a natural wonder that draws visitors from near and far. The Curonian Spit is a haven for outdoor enthusiasts, offering opportunities for hiking, cycling, and birdwatching amidst its pristine landscapes.

Nida, a charming town on the Curonian Spit, is a popular destination within Klaipėda's domain. It's a place where artists and writers have sought inspiration for generations, captivated by the stark beauty of the sand dunes and the tranquil atmosphere. The Thomas Mann House, once the residence of the famous German author, stands as a testament to the area's allure.

Klaipėda's maritime heritage is ever-present, as evidenced by its bustling seaport, one of the largest in the Baltic region. The city's maritime museum, housed in a historic fortress, offers a captivating journey through Lithuania's maritime history, complete with ship models, navigational instruments, and tales of seafaring adventures.

The city's cultural scene is vibrant, with theaters, galleries, and music venues contributing to its lively atmosphere. The annual Klaipėda Castle Jazz Festival draws jazz enthusiasts from across Europe, while the Klaipėda Drama Theatre hosts a range of captivating performances.

Klaipėda's cuisine is a reflection of its coastal location, with an abundance of fresh seafood gracing its menus. Smoked fish, Baltic herring, and seafood chowders are local specialties that celebrate the bounty of the sea. The city's bustling fish market is a sensory delight, where the catch of the day is showcased in all its glory.

Warm and welcoming, Klaipėda is a city that embraces its visitors with open arms. The people here are known for their hospitality and their deep connection to the sea, which has shaped the city's identity for generations.

As you explore Klaipėda, you'll discover a city that bridges the gap between history and modernity, between the allure of the sea and the charm of its streets. It's a place where maritime traditions meet cultural treasures, where natural beauty unfolds at every turn. Klaipėda is Lithuania's seaport gem, a coastal haven that beckons you to explore its shores and immerse yourself in its unique maritime tapestry.

Šiauliai: Exploring Northern Lithuania

Nestled in the northern reaches of Lithuania, Šiauliai is a city that beckons travelers with its unique blend of history, culture, and natural beauty. This vibrant hub in the heart of Northern Lithuania offers a journey through time and landscapes that captivate the senses.

Šiauliai's roots date back to the 13th century when it was founded as a medieval town. Its Old Town, though smaller than those of Vilnius or Kaunas, holds a distinct charm. Narrow streets lead to quaint squares, where centuries-old architecture stands as a testament to the city's enduring heritage. The Church of St. Peter and St. Paul, a Baroque masterpiece, graces the cityscape with its intricate facades and ornate interior.

One of Šiauliai's most iconic landmarks is the Hill of Crosses (Kryžių Kalnas), located just a short drive from the city center. This sacred hill is a place of pilgrimage and reflection, adorned with countless crosses of all sizes and shapes. It's a testament to the resilience and faith of the Lithuanian people, a site that has withstood decades of challenges.

The city's cultural scene thrives, with theaters, galleries, and museums offering a glimpse into Lithuania's artistic heritage. The Šiauliai Art Gallery showcases both contemporary and traditional Lithuanian art, while the Šiauliai Aušros Museum offers insights into the region's history and culture.

Nature enthusiasts will find solace in the surrounding landscapes. The Rūpkalvis Nature Reserve, a short drive from Šiauliai, is a pristine wilderness of forests, lakes, and wetlands. It's a haven for birdwatchers and those seeking to immerse themselves in the tranquility of nature.

Šiauliai is also known for its festivals and events, celebrating everything from music and arts to local traditions. The city comes alive during the Saulės Miestas Festival, a summer celebration that fills the streets with music, dance, and vibrant colors.

As you explore Šiauliai, you'll encounter a city that honors its history, cherishes its cultural heritage, and welcomes visitors with open arms. The people here, known for their warmth and hospitality, are eager to share the stories of their city and the beauty of Northern Lithuania.

In Šiauliai, history whispers through cobblestone streets, nature beckons from its reserves, and culture blooms in galleries and theaters. It's a city that invites you to discover the unique charm of Northern Lithuania, where every corner holds a piece of the nation's rich tapestry. Šiauliai is an exploration of history and beauty, a journey through the heart of Lithuania's northern soul.

The Historic Towns of Trakai and Kernavė

Lithuania, a nation steeped in history, is dotted with charming towns that offer a glimpse into its rich cultural heritage. Two such towns, Trakai and Kernavė, stand as living testaments to the country's past, each with its own unique story to tell.

Trakai, situated just west of the capital, Vilnius, is perhaps best known for its stunning island castle, Trakai Island Castle (Trakų Salos Pilis). This 14th-century fortress is a masterpiece of Gothic architecture, nestled amidst the tranquil waters of Lake Galvė. Its picturesque setting, with wooden footbridges leading to its gates, is the stuff of fairy tales. The castle, once the residence of Lithuanian Grand Dukes, now houses a museum that delves into the history of the region.

Trakai is also celebrated for its multicultural heritage. In the past, it was a gathering place for various ethnic groups, including Lithuanians, Karaites, Tartars, and Jews. Today, the town retains traces of this diversity, with Karaites' wooden houses and the Karaite Kenesa, a place of worship, being notable landmarks.

The town's cuisine is equally diverse, with a focus on dishes that celebrate its lakeside location. Kibinai, savory pastries filled with meat or vegetables, are a local specialty, influenced by the Karaite community. Additionally, freshwater fish, particularly trout and pike, are staples in Trakai's culinary repertoire.

Kernavė, on the other hand, transports visitors back in time to Lithuania's ancient past. This historic town is known as the "Troy of Lithuania" due to its archaeological significance. The Kernavė Archaeological Site, a UNESCO World Heritage site, is a testament to the town's importance as a medieval center of trade and culture.

The town's picturesque hills, known as mounds, are remnants of ancient fortifications that once guarded the Neris River valley. These mounds, including the legendary Mindaugas' Throne Hill, offer panoramic views of the surrounding landscape.

Kernavė is also the site of the annual Joninės (St. John's Day) Festival, a celebration of Lithuanian heritage and Midsummer traditions. During this festival, the town comes alive with folk music, dance, and rituals, giving visitors a taste of the country's vibrant cultural traditions.

Both Trakai and Kernavė provide a window into Lithuania's past, with Trakai showcasing its medieval grandeur and multicultural history, while Kernavė delves into the nation's ancient roots. These historic towns stand as living monuments to Lithuania's enduring spirit and offer a journey through time for those who explore their cobblestone streets and scenic landscapes.

Exploring Lithuania's Rural Beauty

Lithuania, often celebrated for its historic cities and stunning Baltic coastline, also boasts a rural landscape that is nothing short of enchanting. As you venture beyond the urban centers and into the countryside, you'll discover a land characterized by rolling hills, pristine lakes, dense forests, and picturesque villages. It's a journey into a world where time seems to slow down, and the beauty of nature takes center stage.

The Lithuanian countryside is a patchwork of green and gold, with vast expanses of farmland stretching as far as the eye can see. Fields of wheat, barley, and rye sway in the breeze, providing the grains that are the foundation of Lithuanian cuisine. The rural landscape is dotted with quaint farmsteads, where traditional wooden houses stand as a testament to the enduring connection between the people and the land.

Lithuania's rural beauty is also defined by its countless lakes, rivers, and wetlands. Lakes such as Lake Plateliai and Lake Galvė offer opportunities for swimming, boating, and relaxation. The Nemunas River, the country's longest, meanders through the heart of the countryside, carving a path through lush landscapes and offering picturesque views at every turn.

The Dzūkija National Park, one of Lithuania's five national parks, showcases the country's pristine wilderness. Ancient forests, home to diverse flora and fauna, cover much of this region. The park is a haven for hikers and nature enthusiasts, with well-marked trails that lead to serene lakes and remote corners of the woods.

Traditional Lithuanian villages, often nestled amidst this rural beauty, offer a glimpse into the country's cultural heritage. Wooden churches with soaring spires, centuries-old windmills, and roadside shrines dot the landscape, telling stories of faith and tradition. Festivals and events celebrating rural life, such as the Kazlų Rūdos Horse Market, provide an opportunity to immerse oneself in local customs and folklore.

The cuisine in Lithuania's rural areas is hearty and farm-fresh. Dairy products, particularly cheese and curd, play a central role in the diet. Farm-to-table experiences are readily available, with many rural households offering visitors the chance to taste homemade delicacies and learn about traditional food preparation.

Exploring Lithuania's rural beauty is not just a journey through landscapes but a voyage into the heart of a nation. It's an opportunity to connect with the land, savor the simplicity of life, and witness the enduring traditions that have shaped this country for centuries. In the countryside, you'll find a serene and timeless beauty that invites you to slow down, breathe in the fresh air, and savor the essence of Lithuania.

Lithuania's National Parks and Reserves

Lithuania, a country celebrated for its natural beauty, is home to a network of national parks and reserves that protect and showcase the diverse landscapes that define this Baltic nation. From pristine forests to serene lakes and rugged coastlines, these protected areas offer a glimpse into the country's rich biodiversity and its commitment to preserving its natural heritage.

One of Lithuania's most renowned national parks is Curonian Spit National Park (Kuršių Nerijos Nacionalinis Parkas), a UNESCO World Heritage site. Stretching along the Curonian Spit, a unique sandbar separating the Baltic Sea from the Curonian Lagoon, this park is a haven for nature enthusiasts. Its shifting sand dunes, dense pine forests, and serene beaches provide a habitat for diverse wildlife and offer a tranquil escape for visitors.

Dzūkija National Park (Dzūkijos Nacionalinis Parkas), located in the country's southeastern region, is a vast wilderness characterized by ancient woodlands, pristine lakes, and meandering rivers. The park is home to a rich variety of flora and fauna, including the European bison, Lithuania's national symbol. Hikers and nature lovers can explore its well-marked trails, leading to hidden lakes and secluded corners of the forest.

Aukštaitija National Park (Aukštaitijos Nacionalinis Parkas) in the northeast is renowned for its glacially formed landscapes, dotted with numerous lakes and forests. It's a paradise for outdoor activities such as canoeing, hiking, and birdwatching. The park is also home to ethnographic villages that showcase traditional Lithuanian culture and architecture.

Zemaitija National Park (Žemaitijos Nacionalinis Parkas) in the western part of the country encompasses a mosaic of forests, wetlands, and lakes. Lake Plateliai, the largest lake in the park, is a popular destination for water sports and fishing. The park's diverse ecosystems support a wide array of plant and animal species, making it a prime location for wildlife enthusiasts.

Lithuania's national parks and reserves are not only about preserving nature but also about providing educational opportunities. Visitors can learn about the country's natural heritage through interactive exhibits, visitor centers, and guided tours that promote conservation and awareness.

These protected areas are a testament to Lithuania's commitment to safeguarding its natural treasures and fostering an appreciation for the environment. They serve as havens for biodiversity, recreational outlets for the public, and windows into the country's rich ecological tapestry. Exploring Lithuania's national parks and reserves is an invitation to immerse oneself in the beauty and wonder of the natural world, where every step is a journey through pristine landscapes and a celebration of the country's commitment to conservation.

The Curonian Spit: A Natural Wonder

Nestled along Lithuania's western coast, the Curonian Spit stands as one of Europe's most captivating natural wonders. Stretching for approximately 98 kilometers (61 miles) between Lithuania and Russia's Kaliningrad Oblast, this unique sandbar is a masterpiece of nature's artistry, and its story is a testament to the delicate balance between land and sea.

The Curonian Spit is a geological marvel, formed over thousands of years through the intricate dance of wind, water, and sand. Its creation began as glaciers receded, leaving behind vast deposits of sand and sediment. The relentless force of the Baltic Sea currents and winds began shaping this material into the distinctive form we see today.

This slender strip of land, with an average width of just 400 meters (1,312 feet), is home to some of the tallest sand dunes in Europe. The most famous of these, the Parnidis Dune, reaches a staggering height of 52 meters (171 feet) and provides panoramic views of the surrounding landscape, including the peaceful waters of the Curonian Lagoon and the dramatic expanse of the Baltic Sea.

The Curonian Spit's natural beauty extends beyond its dunes. Dense pine forests cover much of the land, providing habitat for a diverse range of flora and fauna. The region is a haven for birdwatchers, with migratory birds using it as a vital stopover point on their journeys. The pristine beaches, with their fine golden sands, draw visitors seeking relaxation and tranquility.

One of the most remarkable features of the Curonian Spit is its shifting sands. The constant movement of dunes, driven by the prevailing winds, creates an ever-changing landscape that challenges the very definition of permanence. Some areas, once inhabited, have been reclaimed by the sands, leaving behind ghostly reminders of human presence.

The region's history is intertwined with its natural beauty. It has been inhabited for centuries, with fishing communities and small villages dotting its shores. The Curonian Spit was also the inspiration for the works of famed German writer Thomas Mann, who spent time in the nearby town of Nida and found creative inspiration in its ethereal landscapes.

Today, the Curonian Spit is not only a natural wonder but also a UNESCO World Heritage site, recognized for its exceptional beauty and ecological significance. It's a place where the forces of nature continue to shape and reshape the land, where every visit unveils a new facet of its timeless allure.

Exploring the Curonian Spit is an invitation to connect with nature in its purest form, to walk in the footsteps of ancient glaciers, and to witness the ever-evolving masterpiece of wind and sand. It's a journey through a land where the boundaries between land and sea blur, and where the relentless forces of nature have crafted a landscape that is as ephemeral as it is breathtaking. The Curonian Spit is a natural wonder that humbles and inspires, a testament to the enduring power of the Earth's creative forces.

Hill of Crosses: A Symbol of Faith

Nestled in the Lithuanian countryside, the Hill of Crosses (Kryžių Kalnas) stands as an iconic symbol of unwavering faith and resilience. This sacred hill, located near the city of Šiauliai, is a place of profound spiritual significance, drawing pilgrims and visitors from around the world who come to witness the sheer magnitude of crosses that cover the landscape.

The history of the Hill of Crosses is as deep as it is poignant. Its origins can be traced back to the 19th century, when the first crosses began to appear on this small but significant hill. These early crosses were often placed by grieving families as a way to remember loved ones lost during uprisings and conflicts, particularly those who never returned home. Over time, the hill became a powerful symbol of Lithuanian identity, resilience, and faith in the face of adversity.

The Hill of Crosses has faced numerous challenges throughout its history. During the Soviet occupation of Lithuania, the site was bulldozed multiple times in an attempt to suppress religious expression and national identity. However, the people of Lithuania and believers from afar continued to rebuild and restore the crosses, refusing to let go of their deeply held beliefs.

Today, the hill is a mesmerizing sight, with an estimated 100,000 crosses of all sizes and materials covering its slopes. These crosses represent not only a testament to faith but also a reflection of personal stories, prayers, and hopes. Pilgrims and visitors often leave their own crosses as a form of devotion, and the result is a landscape that is ever-evolving, reflecting the collective faith of those who visit.

The Hill of Crosses is not tied to any specific religious denomination; rather, it is a place where people of various faiths and backgrounds come to seek solace, offer prayers, and find inspiration. It's a place where the weight of history and the power of faith converge, creating an atmosphere that is both solemn and uplifting.

Visiting the Hill of Crosses is a profoundly moving experience. As you wander among the crosses, each with its own story to tell, you can't help but feel the weight of history and the resilience of the human spirit. The Hill of Crosses is a testament to the enduring power of faith, a symbol of hope in the face of adversity, and a reflection of the deep spirituality that has been woven into the fabric of Lithuania's identity for centuries.

In a world where beliefs and traditions can often seem fleeting, the Hill of Crosses remains an enduring symbol of faith and a place where the human spirit soars. It is a testament to the unbreakable bond between a people and their convictions, a place where crosses stand not as markers of division, but as symbols of unity, strength, and unwavering belief. The Hill of Crosses stands as a symbol of faith that transcends borders and touches the hearts of all who visit.

Lithuania's Architectural Heritage

Lithuania's architectural heritage is a testament to the country's rich history and cultural diversity. From medieval castles to Baroque churches and Art Nouveau masterpieces, Lithuania's architectural landscape is a captivating blend of styles and influences that have shaped the nation's identity over the centuries.

One of the most iconic architectural landmarks in Lithuania is Vilnius Old Town, a UNESCO World Heritage site. This historic city center is a treasure trove of architectural gems, with buildings dating back to the Middle Ages. The Cathedral Basilica of St. Stanislaus and St. Ladislaus, an impressive Gothic masterpiece, is a focal point of the Old Town and a symbol of Lithuania's enduring faith.

The Trakai Island Castle, situated on an island in Lake Galvė, is another architectural gem that transports visitors to the medieval era. This red-brick fortress, surrounded by serene waters, is a symbol of Lithuania's grand ducal history and a testament to its strategic importance.

Lithuania's architectural heritage extends to its churches, reflecting the country's strong Catholic traditions. The Church of St. Peter and St. Paul in Vilnius is a Baroque marvel known for its intricate stucco decorations and impressive frescoes. The Church of St. Anne, a masterpiece of Flamboyant Gothic architecture, is celebrated for its delicate brickwork and intricate façade.

Art Nouveau enthusiasts will find a wealth of treasures in the city of Kaunas. The district of Žaliakalnis is a living gallery of Art Nouveau architecture, with ornate facades, sinuous lines, and decorative details that showcase the artistic flair of the early 20th century.

The country's architectural heritage is not limited to its cities; Lithuania's countryside boasts traditional wooden architecture that is both charming and functional. Wooden churches, with their distinctive tall spires and intricate wooden detailing, are scattered throughout rural Lithuania, offering a glimpse into the country's religious and architectural history.

In the town of Nida on the Curonian Spit, traditional wooden fishermen's cottages known as "Nida-style" houses are a testament to the region's unique architecture. These colorful cottages with thatched roofs reflect the close relationship between the people and the sea.

Lithuania's architectural heritage is a reflection of its enduring spirit, its ability to adapt to changing times, and its pride in preserving its history and culture. Whether you wander through the cobblestone streets of Vilnius Old Town, marvel at the grandeur of medieval castles, or admire the Art Nouveau facades in Kaunas, you are tracing the footsteps of a nation that values its architectural legacy as a bridge to the past and a beacon to the future. Lithuania's architectural heritage is a story of innovation, resilience, and artistic excellence that continues to inspire and captivate those who explore its diverse and captivating landscapes.

Lithuanian Art and Craftsmanship

Lithuania's art and craftsmanship are a testament to the country's rich cultural heritage and creative spirit. Throughout its history, Lithuania has produced talented artists and skilled artisans whose works have left an indelible mark on the world of art.

One of the most celebrated Lithuanian artists is Mikalojus Konstantinas Čiurlionis, a painter and composer who is often regarded as a pioneer of abstract art. His works, characterized by their intricate symbolism and vivid colors, explore the intersection of music and visual art. Čiurlionis' paintings are revered for their spiritual depth and innovation, making him a national icon.

In the realm of literature and poetry, Lithuania boasts literary giants such as Czesław Miłosz, who was of Lithuanian descent and awarded the Nobel Prize in Literature. Miłosz's poetry reflects his deep connection to Lithuania's landscapes and its people, and his writing continues to inspire readers worldwide.

Lithuania's craftsmanship is equally impressive, with a long history of producing high-quality textiles, ceramics, and wooden crafts. Traditional Lithuanian weaving, known as juostos, produces intricate patterns and designs that are both beautiful and meaningful. These textiles are often used in traditional clothing and home decor.

Ceramics in Lithuania have a rich tradition, with distinctive styles like Raudondvaris pottery known for its red clay and unique glazing techniques. The country's pottery traditions have been passed down through generations, resulting in a wide range of functional and artistic ceramics.

Woodworking is another craft that holds a special place in Lithuanian culture. Traditional wooden sculptures, often depicting religious themes or folk motifs, showcase the skill of Lithuanian woodcarvers. These wooden sculptures are found in churches, homes, and outdoor spaces throughout the country.

Contemporary Lithuanian artists and craftsmen continue to push the boundaries of creativity. The capital city, Vilnius, is home to a thriving art scene with numerous galleries and exhibitions showcasing the work of emerging and established artists. Lithuanian designers are gaining recognition for their innovative fashion, furniture, and product design, blending traditional craftsmanship with modern aesthetics.

Lithuania's commitment to preserving and promoting its artistic heritage is evident in its numerous museums and cultural institutions. The Lithuanian Art Museum, located in Vilnius, houses an extensive collection of artworks, including pieces from the Renaissance, Baroque, and modern periods.

Lithuania's art and craftsmanship are not confined to museums and galleries; they are woven into the fabric of everyday life. From traditional craft fairs to contemporary art festivals, the country celebrates its artistic heritage with a sense of pride and dedication.

Exploring Lithuania's art and craftsmanship is an invitation to delve into a world of creativity, tradition, and innovation. Whether you are admiring the works of Čiurlionis, marveling at the intricate patterns of woven textiles, or discovering the beauty of Lithuanian ceramics, you are embarking on a journey through a culture that finds beauty in craftsmanship and expression in art. Lithuania's artistic legacy is a source of inspiration and a testament to the enduring power of human creativity.

Music and Dance in Lithuanian Culture

Lithuanian culture is deeply infused with the rhythms of music and dance, creating a vibrant tapestry that reflects the heart and soul of the nation. From traditional folk melodies to contemporary compositions, from lively dances to solemn rituals, music and dance are integral to the identity of Lithuania.

Folk music holds a special place in Lithuanian culture. The country's rich tradition of polyphonic singing, known as "daina," is recognized by UNESCO as a masterpiece of oral and intangible heritage. Daina encompasses a wide range of songs, from lullabies and work songs to epic narratives, and they are often performed in groups, with each singer contributing to the intricate harmonies.

One of the most celebrated aspects of Lithuanian folk music is its use of multipart singing, where multiple voices blend together to create a hauntingly beautiful sound. These songs often convey themes of love, nature, and the daily life of the people. They have been passed down through generations and are an integral part of Lithuanian celebrations and gatherings.

Traditional musical instruments, such as the kanklės (a type of zither) and the birbyne (a type of hornpipe), add depth and texture to Lithuanian folk music. These instruments have been crafted and played for centuries, and they continue to be cherished for their unique timbres and cultural significance. Dance is another essential element of

Lithuanian culture. Folk dances, often accompanied by live music, are a lively and integral part of celebrations and festivals. These dances vary in style and tempo, from spirited circle dances to elegant partner dances. Many of these dances have specific regional variations, reflecting the diverse cultural landscape of Lithuania. One of the most iconic Lithuanian dances is the "policija" or "broom dance." Dancers twirl brooms with precision and grace, creating intricate patterns and rhythms that are both mesmerizing and joyful. The broom dance is a symbol of unity and coordination, and it is often performed at weddings and other festive occasions.

In addition to traditional folk music and dance, Lithuania has a thriving contemporary music scene. The country has produced talented composers, singers, and musicians who have made their mark on the international stage. Classical music is highly regarded, with Lithuanian composers like Mikalojus Konstantinas Čiurlionis and Juozas Naujalis contributing to the global classical repertoire.

In the realm of popular music, Lithuania has seen the rise of acclaimed artists in various genres, from rock and pop to jazz and electronic music. The Lithuanian Song Festival, held every four years, is a grand celebration of music and culture that brings together thousands of performers and spectators.

Lithuanian culture is a symphony of voices and a whirlwind of movement, where music and dance serve as a means of expression, storytelling, and connection. Whether you find yourself in a bustling city concert hall or a tranquil village gathering, the melodies and rhythms of Lithuania's music and dance will envelop you, inviting you to join in the celebration of a vibrant and enduring cultural heritage.

Festivals and Celebrations in Lithuania

Lithuania's calendar is marked by a vibrant tapestry of festivals and celebrations that reflect the country's rich cultural traditions, religious heritage, and deep sense of community. These gatherings are a testament to the Lithuanian spirit and a window into the heart of this European nation.

One of the most significant and widely celebrated holidays in Lithuania is Easter, known as "Velykos." Easter traditions are deeply rooted in the country's Christian heritage, and the holiday is marked by a variety of customs and rituals. Families come together to paint and decorate eggs, often with intricate designs and vibrant colors. On Easter Sunday, it's customary to attend church services and share a festive meal that includes dishes like "šaltibarščiai" (cold beet soup) and "skruzdėlynas" (a cake resembling an ant hill). It's a time for renewal and joy, and you'll find towns and villages adorned with colorful Easter displays.

Another important religious celebration is Christmas, known as "Kūčios." Lithuanians take great care in preparing for this holiday, with weeks of anticipation leading up to the big day. Families gather for a traditional Christmas Eve meal that includes twelve dishes, representing the twelve apostles. This meal typically consists of fish, mushrooms, sauerkraut, and various desserts. After the meal, it's a tradition to exchange gifts and attend Midnight Mass.

Lithuania's pagan roots are still evident in some of its celebrations, such as "Joninės" or "Rasos," celebrated on the summer solstice. This midsummer festival involves lighting bonfires, singing folk songs, and dancing until the early hours of the morning. People also gather herbs and flowers, believing that they possess special healing powers when picked on this magical night.

One of the most exuberant and widely recognized Lithuanian festivals is "Užgavėnės," the annual Shrove Tuesday celebration. During this pre-Lenten festival, people don masks and costumes and take to the streets to chase away the winter and welcome the arrival of spring. Pancakes, known as "blynai," are a central part of the festivities and are enjoyed in various forms, from sweet to savory.

Lithuania's musical heritage is celebrated during the Lithuanian Song Festival, held every four years. This grand event brings together thousands of singers and spectators, creating a breathtaking spectacle of choral performances and traditional costumes. The festival is a powerful symbol of national identity and unity, showcasing the enduring importance of music in Lithuanian culture.

Throughout the year, Lithuania also hosts numerous music festivals, art exhibitions, and cultural events that showcase both traditional and contemporary expressions of creativity. The Vilnius International Film Festival, known as "Kino Pavasaris," is one of the largest film festivals in the Baltics and draws filmmakers and cinephiles from around the world.

Sports enthusiasts can partake in or watch the traditional "Baltic Way Run," commemorating the historic Baltic Way human chain for independence. Lithuania's love for basketball is also celebrated during the EuroBasket tournament and local league games, where the fervent support of fans creates an electrifying atmosphere.

Lithuania's festivals and celebrations are a reflection of a nation that takes pride in its cultural heritage, values community, and knows how to revel in the joy of life. Whether you're partaking in the solemn rituals of Easter, joining the midsummer bonfires, or dancing through the streets during Užgavėnės, you'll experience the warmth and hospitality that are at the heart of Lithuania's festive spirit.

Religion and Spirituality in Lithuania

Religion has played a profound and enduring role in the history and culture of Lithuania. The nation's spiritual journey is marked by a diverse tapestry of beliefs, customs, and traditions, reflecting both its Christian heritage and ancient pagan roots.

Christianity was introduced to Lithuania in the late 14th century, with the baptism of Grand Duke Jogaila, who later became King Władysław II Jagiełło of Poland. This marked the beginning of the country's conversion to Christianity, primarily adopting Roman Catholicism. The Christian faith quickly became intertwined with Lithuanian identity, and Catholicism remains the dominant religion in the country to this day.

The Catholic Church has played a central role in shaping Lithuania's spiritual and cultural landscape. The country boasts numerous beautiful churches and cathedrals, many of which are adorned with exquisite artwork and architectural details. Vilnius, the capital, is often called the "Rome of the North" due to its abundance of churches and religious institutions.

One of Lithuania's most significant religious sites is the Hill of Crosses, located near the city of Šiauliai. This sacred hill is covered in thousands of crosses, large and small, left by pilgrims as expressions of faith and hope. It has become a symbol of resilience and determination, surviving attempts to remove it during times of political oppression.

The Christian calendar is marked by a series of religious festivals and celebrations, including Easter and Christmas. These holidays are observed with great reverence and are often accompanied by traditional rituals and customs. Christmas Eve, known as "Kūčios," is a particularly cherished holiday when families gather for a festive meal and the exchange of gifts.

Despite the prevalence of Christianity, Lithuania has also retained some of its pagan traditions, particularly in its celebrations of the natural world. Midsummer's Eve, known as "Rasos" or "Joninės," is a celebration of the summer solstice and is marked by bonfires, singing, and the gathering of herbs and flowers believed to possess special powers.

In addition to Catholicism, other Christian denominations such as Protestantism and Eastern Orthodoxy are also practiced in Lithuania, contributing to the religious diversity of the nation. Additionally, a small Jewish community has deep historical roots in Lithuania, although the Holocaust and emigration significantly impacted its size.

In recent years, there has been a resurgence of interest in ancient Baltic pagan traditions. Some Lithuanians explore their pre-Christian heritage through rituals, festivals, and the revival of ancient beliefs associated with nature and the seasons.

Lithuania's commitment to religious freedom and tolerance is enshrined in its constitution. The nation values the coexistence of various religious and spiritual beliefs, fostering an atmosphere of respect and harmony among its diverse communities.

Religion and spirituality continue to be an integral part of Lithuania's cultural fabric. Whether attending a Catholic Mass in a centuries-old cathedral, participating in the colorful traditions of Easter, or honoring the timeless traditions of Rasos, Lithuania's spiritual journey is a testament to the enduring power of faith and the rich tapestry of beliefs that shape its identity.

Folklore and Mythology: Tales of Lithuania

Lithuania's folklore and mythology are a treasure trove of ancient wisdom, enchanting tales, and timeless legends that have been passed down through generations. These stories provide a glimpse into the collective imagination of the Lithuanian people and reveal their deep connection to the natural world and their unique cultural identity.

At the heart of Lithuanian folklore are the "dainos," traditional folk songs that have been recognized by UNESCO as a masterpiece of oral and intangible heritage. These songs are not only poetic expressions of everyday life but also repositories of ancient wisdom, legends, and myths. The dainos are often sung in multipart harmony, creating a mesmerizing and hauntingly beautiful sound.

One of the central figures in Lithuanian folklore is the mythical character of "Eglė the Queen of Serpents." Eglė is a young and fearless queen who marries a serpent prince and embarks on a series of adventures filled with magic and wonder. This tale embodies themes of transformation, love, and the interplay between the human and natural worlds.

Another beloved character is "Jūratė the Sea Goddess." According to Lithuanian mythology, Jūratė resides in an underwater palace made of amber and rules over the Baltic Sea. Her story revolves around forbidden love with a mortal fisherman named Kastytis and the tragic consequences that ensue. The legend of Jūratė and Kastytis reflects the reverence and awe that Lithuanians have for the Baltic Sea and its mysteries.

Lithuania's folklore is rich with stories of mythical creatures and spirits. The "Laukynė" are woodland spirits that protect the forests and the creatures that inhabit them. "Laume" are benevolent female spirits who watch over children and ensure their well-being. These spirits are deeply rooted in the belief in the interconnectedness of all living beings and the need for harmony with the natural world.

The "Ragana," or witch, is another intriguing figure in Lithuanian folklore. Unlike the malevolent witches of some European traditions, the Lithuanian Ragana often possesses wisdom and knowledge of herbs and healing. She plays a vital role in folk tales, offering guidance and assistance to those in need.

In addition to traditional folk tales, Lithuanian mythology also includes the concept of "Dievai," the gods of the Baltic pantheon. These gods are associated with natural forces and elements, such as the god of thunder, Perkūnas, and the goddess of the earth, Žemyna. These deities reflect the deep spiritual connection that Lithuanians have with the land, the sky, and the elements.

Lithuania's folklore and mythology are a testament to the enduring power of storytelling and the importance of preserving cultural heritage. These tales continue to be celebrated through festivals, performances, and artistic expressions, reminding the Lithuanian people of their rich and unique cultural identity.

Modern Lithuanian Literature and Writers

Modern Lithuanian literature is a testament to the nation's enduring passion for storytelling, artistic expression, and the power of words. This literary tradition, deeply rooted in the country's history and culture, has produced a wealth of talented writers whose works resonate with both local and international audiences.

One of the towering figures in modern Lithuanian literature is Czesław Miłosz, a poet and essayist who was born in Lithuania but wrote primarily in Polish. Miłosz received the Nobel Prize in Literature in 1980 for his powerful and thought-provoking works, which often grappled with the complexities of identity, history, and the human condition. His writings, including "The Captive Mind" and "The Issa Valley," continue to be widely read and admired.

Vincas Mykolaitis-Putinas, a prominent Lithuanian writer of the early 20th century, is known for his novel "Altorių Šešėly" (In the Shadow of the Altars). This work caused significant controversy due to its exploration of religious and moral themes. Mykolaitis-Putinas's literary contributions also extended to poetry and essays, making him a versatile and influential figure in Lithuanian literature. The 20th century was a period of great turbulence for Lithuania, marked by occupations and political upheaval. During this time, writers like Antanas Škėma emerged, addressing the challenges of modernity and existentialism. Škėma's novel "Balta drobulė" (The White Shroud) is a masterpiece that delves into the psychological struggles of its protagonist and is considered a cornerstone of Lithuanian literature.

Sigitas Parulskis, a contemporary writer, has gained recognition for his thought-provoking novels and poetry. His works often explore philosophical and ethical questions, challenging readers to contemplate the complexities of the modern world. Parulskis has received numerous literary awards for his contributions to Lithuanian literature.

Undoubtedly, the literary scene in Lithuania is not limited to a few renowned figures. It is a vibrant and dynamic landscape with a diverse array of voices, genres, and themes. From poets like Judita Vaičiūnaitė, who captured the beauty of everyday life, to prose writers like Jurga Ivanauskaitė, whose works dealt with taboo subjects, modern Lithuanian literature reflects the nation's ever-evolving identity and its response to the challenges of the contemporary world.

The Lithuanian language, with its rich history and linguistic nuances, continues to be a source of inspiration for writers who seek to explore the depths of human experience and emotion. Whether addressing the complexities of identity, the impact of history, or the universal themes of love and loss, modern Lithuanian literature remains a vital and vibrant part of the global literary landscape.

In a world where literature has the power to transcend borders and connect people across cultures, modern Lithuanian writers have contributed their unique voices to the global conversation, enriching the tapestry of world literature with their stories, insights, and artistic prowess.

The Resilience of the Lithuanian Language

The Lithuanian language, with its ancient roots and remarkable resilience, stands as a testament to the enduring spirit of the Lithuanian people. It is a language that has weathered centuries of historical challenges, invasions, and political changes, emerging as a symbol of national identity and cultural pride.

At its core, the Lithuanian language belongs to the Baltic branch of the Indo-European language family, which makes it one of the oldest languages still spoken in Europe today. Its linguistic heritage can be traced back to the early medieval period, making it a linguistic treasure trove for scholars and linguists alike.

One of the defining features of the Lithuanian language is its archaic nature. It has retained many linguistic characteristics and vocabulary elements that have disappeared from other Indo-European languages over time. This linguistic conservatism has made Lithuanian an invaluable resource for researchers studying the evolution of languages.

The resilience of the Lithuanian language can be attributed in part to the enduring commitment of the Lithuanian people to preserve their linguistic heritage. Despite periods of foreign rule and suppression, Lithuanians have steadfastly maintained their language and culture, using it as a tool for resistance and resilience.

A pivotal moment in the history of the Lithuanian language came with the publication of the first Lithuanian book, the Catechism by Martynas Mažvydas, in 1547. This event marked the beginning of Lithuanian-language literature and played a crucial role in the development of written Lithuanian. It also contributed to the preservation of the language during challenging times.

The 19th century saw a resurgence of interest in the Lithuanian language and culture, often referred to as the Lithuanian National Revival. Scholars and writers like Jonas Jablonskis and Antanas Baranauskas played key roles in standardizing and modernizing the language. Their efforts laid the foundation for the contemporary Lithuanian language as we know it today.

The Lithuanian language faced significant challenges during the periods of foreign rule, particularly under Russian and Soviet occupation. However, Lithuanians continued to use their language as a form of resistance and a symbol of national pride. It was during these times that the importance of preserving the language became even more apparent.

Since Lithuania regained its independence in 1990, the Lithuanian language has experienced a renaissance. It is now the official language of the country, and efforts have been made to promote its use in education, government, and media. Lithuanian language courses are widely available, and language revitalization initiatives have been successful in instilling a sense of pride and ownership among younger generations.

In the modern era, the Lithuanian language faces new challenges posed by globalization and the dominance of

English as a global lingua franca. However, Lithuanians remain committed to preserving their linguistic heritage. The resilience of the Lithuanian language serves as a reminder that languages are not static entities but living expressions of culture, history, and identity.

Language Revival and Preservation Efforts

Lithuania's commitment to preserving its language is nothing short of inspiring. The Lithuanian language, one of the oldest in Europe, holds a special place in the hearts of its people, and efforts to ensure its continued existence have been ongoing for centuries.

Historical Background: The roots of language preservation in Lithuania can be traced back to the 19th century when the country was under foreign rule. During this time, Lithuanian intellectuals and scholars recognized the importance of safeguarding their language and culture. They understood that language was not merely a means of communication but a vessel for preserving the nation's identity.

One significant milestone was the publication of the first Lithuanian-language newspaper, "Aušra" (Dawn), in 1883. It played a pivotal role in promoting the use of the Lithuanian language and fostering a sense of national unity.

Language Suppression: However, the road to language preservation was fraught with challenges. Lithuania endured periods of foreign domination, including Russian and Soviet rule, which aimed to suppress Lithuanian culture and language in favor of the dominant powers. During these times, speaking, writing, or teaching in the Lithuanian language was often met with severe consequences.

Soviet Rule and Resilience: The Soviet occupation of Lithuania from 1940 to 1990 posed a particularly grave threat to the Lithuanian language. The Soviets attempted to Russify Lithuania by imposing the Russian language in schools and official institutions. Despite these efforts, Lithuanians demonstrated remarkable resilience in safeguarding their language. Secret gatherings, underground publications, and oral traditions were vital in keeping the language alive.

Independence and Language Renewal: Lithuania's restoration of independence in 1990 marked a turning point for the language. It allowed for the full-fledged revival of Lithuanian as the official language of the country. Educational institutions, government bodies, and cultural organizations made concerted efforts to promote and teach the language.

The Lithuanian Language Commission, established in 1990, has been instrumental in standardizing and preserving the language. It ensures that Lithuanian remains a living and evolving language, capable of adapting to contemporary needs while staying true to its roots.

Language Preservation Initiatives: Lithuania has also made significant efforts to teach Lithuanian to its diaspora communities around the world. Initiatives like the "Lithuanian Heritage Schools" program aim to connect young Lithuanians abroad with their language and cultural heritage.

Modern Challenges: Despite these commendable efforts, modern challenges persist. The digital age has brought new dimensions to language preservation. While technology provides opportunities for language learning and dissemination, it also presents the challenge of digital content in dominant languages overshadowing the use of Lithuanian.

Lithuania's commitment to preserving and revitalizing its language is a testament to the nation's deep cultural roots and resilience. It is a remarkable story of how a people can fight against adversity to protect their linguistic heritage. The ongoing efforts to ensure the survival and prosperity of the Lithuanian language continue to be a source of pride and inspiration for the nation.

Learning Lithuanian: Tips and Resources

Learning a new language is a rewarding journey, and when that language is Lithuanian, you're delving into a unique linguistic world with a rich history. Whether you're planning a trip to Lithuania, connecting with your Lithuanian heritage, or simply embracing the joy of language learning, here are some valuable tips and resources to help you along the way.

1. **Start with the Basics:**
   - Begin by mastering the Lithuanian alphabet and pronunciation. Understanding the sounds of the language is essential for effective communication.
2. **Online Courses and Apps:**
   - Numerous language learning apps and websites offer Lithuanian courses. Duolingo, Memrise, and Babbel are popular choices. These interactive platforms provide structured lessons and exercises.
3. **Language Classes:**
   - If you prefer a more traditional approach, consider enrolling in a language class. Many universities and language schools around the world offer Lithuanian courses.
4. **Language Exchange Partners:**
   - Find a language exchange partner who speaks Lithuanian and is learning your native language. This can be an enjoyable way to practice conversational skills.

5. **Immerse Yourself:**
   o If possible, spend time in Lithuania or in Lithuanian-speaking communities. Immersion is one of the most effective ways to learn any language.
6. **Online Resources:**
   o Explore online resources like YouTube channels, podcasts, and blogs dedicated to teaching Lithuanian. These often include lessons, cultural insights, and pronunciation guides.
7. **Lithuanian Literature and Media:**
   o Reading Lithuanian books, newspapers, and watching Lithuanian films or TV shows can improve your comprehension and vocabulary.
8. **Lithuanian Language Schools:**
   o Consider attending a language school in Lithuania for an intensive learning experience. These programs often offer cultural activities alongside language classes.
9. **Language Tutors:**
   o Hiring a private tutor can provide personalized instruction and guidance tailored to your learning style and goals.
10. **Language Meetup Groups:**
    o Join local language meetup groups or online communities where you can practice Lithuanian with native speakers and fellow learners.
11. **Dictionaries and Language Apps:**
    o Download Lithuanian-English or Lithuanian-language dictionaries and apps for quick reference and vocabulary building.

12. Persistence and Patience:

- o Learning a new language takes time and effort. Be patient with yourself and stay consistent in your practice.

13. Cultural Understanding:

- o To truly appreciate the language, take time to understand Lithuanian culture, history, and traditions. This will enhance your language learning experience.

14. Government Resources:

- o Some Lithuanian government agencies and cultural institutions offer language learning materials and resources for free.

15. Celebrate Milestones:

- o Celebrate your achievements along the way, whether it's mastering a new set of vocabulary or successfully holding a conversation. Recognizing progress keeps you motivated.

Remember that language learning is a personal journey, and the key is to enjoy the process. Embrace the beauty of the Lithuanian language, connect with its culture, and open doors to new experiences and connections. Learning Lithuanian is not just about words; it's about understanding and becoming a part of a vibrant and unique linguistic heritage.

Lithuanian Traditions and Etiquette

When exploring the culture of Lithuania, it's essential to understand and appreciate the rich tapestry of traditions and etiquette that shape daily life and social interactions in this Baltic nation. Here, we delve into some key aspects of Lithuanian traditions and etiquette that will help you navigate and connect with this vibrant culture.

Hospitality and Warmth: Lithuanians are known for their warm hospitality. When visiting someone's home, it's customary to bring a small gift, such as flowers or chocolates, as a token of appreciation. When invited, it's polite to accept the offer and remove your shoes upon entering the host's home.

Greetings and Formalities: When meeting someone for the first time, a firm handshake and direct eye contact are common greetings. Addressing people with their title and last name is considered respectful. While Lithuanians are generally informal, maintaining politeness is important.

Gift Giving: Giving and receiving gifts is an integral part of Lithuanian culture. Special occasions like birthdays, name days, and holidays are opportunities to exchange gifts. Thoughtfulness in choosing a gift is highly valued.

Name Days: Name days hold significant importance in Lithuania. Each day of the year is associated with specific names, and people celebrate their name day as if it were their birthday. Congratulating someone on their name day is a sign of respect.

Dining Etiquette: Lithuanian cuisine is a treasure trove of flavors and traditions. When dining with locals, it's customary to wait for the host's invitation before starting the meal. Complimenting the cook is considered polite. It's also important to finish your plate as a sign of appreciation.

Religious Traditions: Lithuania has a strong Catholic heritage, and religious holidays like Easter and Christmas are celebrated with fervor. Attending church services during these times is common, and participating in traditional rituals, like the Easter egg tapping game, is part of the experience.

Midsummer's Eve (Joninės or Rasos): This ancient pagan celebration takes place on June 24th and is a time for bonfires, dancing, and singing. Traditional wreaths of flowers are made and worn, and it's a time when people connect with nature and celebrate the longest day of the year.

Respect for Nature: Lithuanians have a deep respect for nature and the environment. Activities like mushroom picking and berry gathering are cherished traditions, and the Lithuanian countryside is a place where many find solace and connection to their roots.

Singing Revolution: Music, particularly choral singing, plays a crucial role in Lithuanian culture. The "Singing Revolution" was a pivotal moment in the country's history when singing and peaceful protests helped lead to independence from the Soviet Union.

Language and Pride: The Lithuanian language is a source of national pride and identity. Efforts to preserve and promote the language are ongoing, making it a significant part of daily life.

As you engage with Lithuanian culture, keep in mind that while traditions are essential, the people of Lithuania are also open to new experiences and connections. Embrace the warmth, explore the customs, and be prepared to immerse yourself in a culture that is proud of its heritage and welcomes those who appreciate its traditions and etiquette.

The Importance of Family in Lithuanian Culture

Family lies at the heart of Lithuanian culture, serving as the cornerstone of society and identity. To understand Lithuania fully, one must appreciate the profound significance that family holds in the lives of its people.

Multigenerational Living: It's common for multiple generations of a family to live under one roof. This practice fosters close bonds between grandparents, parents, and children. It's not unusual for grandparents to actively participate in raising their grandchildren, sharing their wisdom and life experiences.

Strong Family Ties: Lithuanians maintain strong emotional connections with their extended families. Family gatherings are frequent, and special occasions are celebrated collectively. These gatherings are opportunities to reinforce family bonds and pass down traditions from one generation to the next.

Support System: Families in Lithuania are not just social units; they are support systems. In times of need or crisis, relatives come together to provide financial, emotional, and practical assistance. This safety net is highly valued and helps individuals face life's challenges with confidence.

Naming Traditions: Naming traditions in Lithuania also reflect the importance of family. Children are often named after grandparents or other relatives, ensuring a connection to the family's history and heritage. This practice keeps the memory of ancestors alive in the present.

Family Celebrations: Family celebrations, such as weddings and christenings, are elaborate affairs. They are marked by traditions, rituals, and feasting, bringing extended families and friends together to celebrate joyous occasions. These events are a testament to the role family plays in creating lasting memories.

Legacy and Heritage: Passing down family traditions, stories, and values is a crucial aspect of Lithuanian culture. Families take pride in preserving their heritage and ensuring that future generations carry forward the knowledge and customs that define their identity.

Elders and Wisdom: Elders hold a special place in Lithuanian families. Their wisdom and life experiences are respected and sought after. They often serve as mentors and role models for younger family members, contributing to their personal growth and development.

Care for the Elderly: Lithuanian families traditionally care for their elderly relatives at home, rather than sending them to nursing homes. This practice demonstrates the deep respect and love that families have for their older members.

Influence on Society: The importance of family extends beyond the home. It influences societal values and norms, emphasizing the significance of unity, mutual support, and a sense of belonging. These values contribute to a strong and resilient society.

Adaptation and Change: While traditional family values remain strong, Lithuanian families, like those elsewhere, are also evolving. Factors such as urbanization and modernization are influencing family dynamics, with some individuals choosing more independent lifestyles.

In essence, family is the cornerstone of Lithuanian culture, providing a sense of identity, belonging, and support. The deeply rooted traditions and values associated with family life have played a pivotal role in shaping Lithuania's rich cultural heritage and continue to be an integral part of its society today.

Lithuanian Hospitality: Welcoming Visitors

Lithuanians take great pride in their tradition of hospitality, which is deeply ingrained in their culture. When you visit Lithuania, you'll quickly discover that the warmth and friendliness of its people are among the country's greatest assets.

Genuine Warmth: Lithuanians are known for their genuine warmth and friendliness toward visitors. Whether you're in the bustling capital city of Vilnius, the historic town of Kaunas, or a quaint rural village, you're likely to encounter welcoming smiles and open hearts.

Guests are Honored: In Lithuanian culture, guests are highly esteemed and considered a blessing. It's not uncommon for hosts to go to great lengths to make their guests feel comfortable and cherished. You'll often be greeted with open arms and offered a place at the family table.

Hospitality Traditions: Traditional Lithuanian hospitality involves offering guests homemade treats and refreshments. You may be served fresh bread with honey, homemade pastries, or a glass of mead, a traditional Lithuanian beverage. These gestures symbolize the host's genuine desire to make you feel at home.

Sharing a Meal: Sharing a meal with your hosts is a common way to experience Lithuanian hospitality. It's an opportunity to connect, share stories, and learn about each other's cultures. Traditional Lithuanian dishes, such as cepelinai (potato dumplings), kugelis (potato pudding), and šaltibarščiai (cold beet soup), are often prepared with love and pride.

Cultural Exchange: Lithuanians are curious about other cultures, and they often appreciate learning from their guests. Be prepared to share your own customs and traditions, as this can lead to enriching cultural exchanges.

Offering Assistance: Lithuanians are also known for their willingness to help visitors. If you're lost or in need of directions, don't hesitate to ask a local for assistance. They'll likely go out of their way to guide you or offer helpful advice.

Respect for Privacy: While Lithuanians are generous hosts, they also respect your privacy. If you need some personal time or space, feel free to communicate your preferences, and your hosts will understand.

Seasonal Festivities: If you visit Lithuania during a holiday or festival, you're in for a treat. These occasions often involve lively celebrations, traditional music, and dance, providing a unique opportunity to experience Lithuanian culture at its most vibrant.

Language Barrier: While English is commonly spoken in urban areas, you may encounter some language barriers in rural parts of the country. Learning a few basic Lithuanian phrases can be a wonderful way to show respect for the local culture and enhance your travel experience.

In conclusion, when you visit Lithuania, you're not just exploring a beautiful country; you're entering a world of warm, heartfelt hospitality. The Lithuanian people's dedication to making visitors feel like cherished guests is a testament to their rich cultural heritage and their genuine love for sharing it with others.

Lithuanian Souvenirs and Craft Markets

When you explore Lithuania, you'll discover a vibrant world of souvenirs and craft markets that reflect the country's rich cultural heritage and craftsmanship. From intricate handwoven textiles to unique wooden carvings, these treasures make for meaningful keepsakes of your Lithuanian journey.

Amber: Lithuania is famous for its amber, often referred to as "Baltic gold." Amber is a fossilized resin found along the Baltic Sea coast, and it has been cherished for centuries. You'll find an array of amber jewelry, from simple pendants to intricately designed bracelets and necklaces, in various shades, from golden honey to deep cognac.

Linen Products: Lithuanian linen is renowned for its quality and durability. Linen textiles, including tablecloths, napkins, and clothing items, are often available in craft markets. Linen is known for its natural cooling properties, making it a perfect choice for warm summer days.

Traditional Textiles: Handwoven textiles play a significant role in Lithuanian culture. Look for rugs, blankets, and clothing items made using traditional weaving techniques. The patterns and colors often hold cultural significance, and each piece tells a story.

Wooden Crafts: Lithuania has a strong tradition of woodwork. You'll come across a variety of wooden crafts, such as intricately carved spoons, bowls, and figurines.

These pieces often feature intricate designs inspired by nature and folklore.

Ceramics: Lithuanian ceramics showcase intricate designs and patterns, including motifs from the region's rich history. You can find ceramic tableware, decorative tiles, and unique pottery items in craft markets.

Amber Jewelry: In addition to raw amber, you'll find a wide selection of amber jewelry, including rings, earrings, and brooches. The craftsmanship and quality make Lithuanian amber jewelry a sought-after souvenir.

Traditional Clothing: While less common, some craft markets may offer traditional Lithuanian clothing, such as woolen vests, skirts, and aprons. These garments often feature intricate embroidery and are a testament to the country's cultural heritage.

Basketry: Lithuanian basketry is a true art form. Skilled artisans create baskets of various shapes and sizes using natural materials like willow and straw. These baskets serve both practical and decorative purposes.

Local Food Products: Some craft markets also feature local food products. Look for jars of honey, homemade preserves, and unique Lithuanian snacks that you can enjoy during your stay or take home as gifts.

Flea Markets: In addition to craft markets, Lithuania has flea markets where you can find a diverse range of vintage and antique items. These markets are treasure troves for collectors and those interested in historical artifacts.

Supporting Local Artisans: When you purchase souvenirs and crafts at these markets, you're not just acquiring beautiful items; you're also supporting local artisans and preserving Lithuania's rich cultural heritage.

Haggling: While haggling is not common in most Lithuanian markets, it's still a good idea to be polite and respectful when negotiating prices, especially in flea markets.

Exploring Lithuanian craft markets is an opportunity to immerse yourself in the country's culture, meet local artisans, and take home unique mementos that encapsulate the spirit of Lithuania. Whether you're searching for a special gift or simply want to treasure the memories of your visit, these markets offer a world of fascinating finds.

Exploring Lithuania Through the Seasons

Lithuania, with its distinct seasons, offers a captivating experience for travelers throughout the year. Each season brings its own unique charm and a range of activities to enjoy. Let's embark on a journey through the Lithuanian seasons, from the frosty winters to the vibrant summers.

Winter: Lithuanian winters are a time of enchantment. The landscape is blanketed in snow, transforming the country into a winter wonderland. The frozen lakes and rivers provide opportunities for ice skating and ice fishing. Winter sports enthusiasts can hit the slopes at one of Lithuania's ski resorts, such as Druskininkai or Anykščiai. The cozy atmosphere of Vilnius, the capital, is perfect for enjoying hot mulled wine and exploring the charming Christmas markets.

Spring: As winter fades away, Lithuania awakens with the arrival of spring. The countryside bursts into bloom with wildflowers, and the parks and forests are a vibrant green. Spring is an ideal time for hiking and exploring Lithuania's natural beauty. You can witness storks returning to their nests and migratory birds passing through. The Easter traditions in Lithuania are deeply rooted in culture, with beautifully decorated eggs and traditional dishes like sakotis, a tree-shaped cake.

Summer: Lithuanian summers are a time of celebration and outdoor activities. The Baltic Sea coastline comes alive with beachgoers, and the Curonian Spit is a haven for sunseekers. Lithuania boasts numerous lakes, making it a popular destination for swimming, boating, and water sports. Festivals abound during the summer, celebrating music, culture, and local traditions. One of the most famous is the Joninės or Rasos festival, celebrating the summer solstice with bonfires and wreath making.

Autumn: As summer fades into autumn, Lithuania's forests turn into a symphony of colors. The golden hues of the leaves create a picturesque backdrop for hiking and exploring. Mushroom picking is a beloved autumn activity, and you'll find locals foraging for a variety of edible mushrooms. The Lithuanian cuisine shifts to hearty dishes like potato pancakes and mushroom soup, perfect for warming up on cool autumn days.

Seasonal Delicacies: Throughout the year, Lithuanian cuisine adapts to the seasons. In winter, try hearty dishes like cepelinai, potato dumplings filled with meat or cheese. Spring brings fresh greens and nettle soup. Summer is the time for cold beet soup and grilled meats, while autumn features rich mushroom dishes and apple-filled desserts.

Nature and Wildlife: Lithuania's diverse landscapes are home to a variety of wildlife. In spring and autumn, you might spot deer and wild boar in the forests. Birdwatching is excellent year-round, with a chance to see eagles, owls, and migratory birds passing through.

Festivals and Celebrations: Lithuanians embrace their seasons with numerous festivals and celebrations. From the magical Christmas markets to the Midsummer's Eve festivities, these events offer insights into local traditions and culture.

Local Insights: Engaging with locals during each season can provide valuable insights. Whether it's learning the art of making traditional Christmas ornaments or joining in a summer solstice celebration, interacting with Lithuanians adds depth to your experience.

Exploring Lithuania through the seasons is a journey filled with natural beauty, cultural richness, and a deep connection to the rhythm of life in this Baltic nation. Whether you prefer the snowy tranquility of winter or the lively festivities of summer, Lithuania offers a unique experience year-round.

Planning Your Trip to Lithuania: Practical Tips

Lithuania, with its rich history, natural beauty, and vibrant culture, is a gem waiting to be explored. Whether you're a seasoned traveler or embarking on your first international adventure, planning a trip to Lithuania can be an exciting endeavor. Here, we'll provide you with practical tips to ensure your journey is smooth, enjoyable, and culturally enriching.

Travel Documents and Visa: Before heading to Lithuania, make sure your passport is valid for at least six months beyond your planned departure date. Most travelers from the United States, Canada, and European Union countries can enter Lithuania visa-free for up to 90 days within a 180-day period. However, it's essential to check the most up-to-date visa requirements for your nationality on Lithuania's official government website or contact the nearest Lithuanian embassy or consulate.

Currency and Money Matters: The official currency of Lithuania is the Euro (EUR). Credit cards are widely accepted in urban areas, but it's advisable to carry some cash, especially when venturing into rural or remote regions. ATMs are readily available throughout the country.

Language: The official language of Lithuania is Lithuanian, a Baltic language with a unique linguistic heritage. While English is spoken and understood, especially in tourist areas and by the younger generation, learning a few basic Lithuanian phrases can go a long way in enhancing your travel experience and earning local appreciation.

Weather and Packing: Lithuania experiences distinct seasons, so pack accordingly based on the time of your visit. Summers can be warm and pleasant, while winters can be cold and snowy. Layered clothing is advisable, along with comfortable walking shoes and, if you're visiting in winter, warm outerwear.

Local Cuisine: Lithuanian cuisine offers a delightful array of dishes, often featuring potatoes, dairy, and meats. Don't miss trying traditional Lithuanian dishes like cepelinai (potato dumplings), šaltibarščiai (cold beet soup), and kugelis (potato pudding). Lithuania also has a thriving craft beer scene, so sample some local brews.

Transportation: Lithuania has a well-developed transportation network. The capital city, Vilnius, has an international airport, while Kaunas and Palanga also offer international flights. Within the country, you can travel by train, bus, or car rental. Trains are efficient and connect major cities, while buses serve smaller towns and rural areas. It's wise to check schedules and book tickets in advance for popular routes.

Safety: Lithuania is generally a safe country for travelers. Like any other destination, be aware of your surroundings, safeguard your belongings, and take common-sense precautions. Emergency services can be reached by dialing 112.

Cultural Etiquette: Lithuanians are known for their warmth and hospitality. It's customary to greet people with a friendly "Labas" (hello) and a handshake. Removing your shoes when entering someone's home is a sign of respect. When visiting churches and religious sites, dress modestly, covering shoulders and knees.

Electrical Outlets: Lithuania uses the European-style Type F electrical outlets, with a standard voltage of 230V and a frequency of 50Hz. Travelers from North America or countries with different plug types may need a travel adapter.

Time Zone: Lithuania operates on Eastern European Time (EET), which is UTC+2 in standard time and UTC+3 during daylight saving time (from the last Sunday in March to the last Sunday in October).

Health and Insurance: Ensure you have comprehensive travel insurance that covers medical expenses and emergencies. The tap water in Lithuania is safe to drink, but if you have any concerns, bottled water is widely available.

Planning your trip to Lithuania involves a blend of practical preparations and a spirit of adventure. By considering these tips and immersing yourself in the culture, you're poised to have an enriching experience in this Baltic nation, filled with memorable moments and new discoveries. Enjoy your journey!

Epilogue

As we conclude our journey through the diverse tapestry of Lithuania, it's worth reflecting on the enduring spirit and unique identity of this Baltic nation. Lithuania, a land of deep forests, serene lakes, and rich traditions, has left an indelible mark on both its people and the world.

The story of Lithuania is one of resilience and determination. From its ancient pagan roots to the Christian conversion in the late 14th century, Lithuania has continuously evolved, embracing change while preserving its cultural heritage. The Grand Duchy of Lithuania, a medieval powerhouse that once rivaled the largest European states, laid the foundation for the Lithuanian identity we see today.

The union with Poland in the 16th century, known as the Polish-Lithuanian Commonwealth, brought about a period of cultural exchange and mutual influence, shaping the artistic and intellectual landscapes of both nations. The Lithuanian Renaissance was a flourishing era of literature, arts, and architecture, with the likes of Mikalojus Daukša and Mikalojus Konstantinas Čiurlionis leaving a lasting legacy.

The Russian Empire's dominance in the 19th century marked a challenging period for Lithuania, as its language and culture faced suppression. However, the resilience of the Lithuanian people eventually led to the restoration of independence in 1918, followed by a tumultuous interwar period.

The impact of World War II and the subsequent Soviet occupation left scars that would take decades to heal. The Baltic Way, a peaceful protest in 1989, was a pivotal moment in Lithuania's history, leading to its ultimate declaration of independence in 1990. The nation had regained its freedom.

Modern Lithuania has emerged as a European nation, embracing democracy, human rights, and economic development. It has made significant strides in preserving its language, culture, and traditions. Lithuanian cuisine has gained international recognition, with its unique dishes and hearty flavors winning the hearts of food enthusiasts worldwide.

Nature's beauty, from the Curonian Spit to the enchanting national parks, continues to attract visitors seeking tranquility and adventure. The Hill of Crosses stands as a testament to the unwavering faith of the Lithuanian people.

Lithuania's architectural heritage, a blend of Gothic, Renaissance, and Baroque styles, graces its towns and cities. Its art and craftsmanship, music and dance, festivals and celebrations, all contribute to a vibrant cultural tapestry.

Language revival efforts have been instrumental in preserving the Lithuanian language, one of the oldest in Europe. Its alphabet, pronunciation, and unique linguistic features reflect centuries of history.

As we conclude our exploration, we leave you with the knowledge that Lithuania, a nation with a deep-rooted love for its land, language, and culture, continues to evolve and shape its future. Its traditions and customs, its welcoming spirit, and the warmth of its people make Lithuania a destination worth discovering.

May your understanding of this remarkable nation inspire your own adventures and foster a deeper appreciation for the diverse world we share. Lithuania, with its past, present, and future, invites you to explore its wonders and be a part of its ongoing story.

Printed in Great Britain
by Amazon

Embark on an enthralling literary adventure through the captivating landscapes, rich traditions, and vibrant culture of Lithuania with "Lithuania: Everything You Need to Know." This text-only masterpiece is a comprehensive exploration of one of Europe's hidden gems, designed to transport you to the heart of this Baltic nation from the comfort of your own reading nook.

+ Discover a Nation's Tale: Delve deep into the storied history of Lithuania, from its ancient pagan origins to its emergence as a European powerhouse, and witness the resilience of its people throughout centuries of change.

+ Journey Through Time: Roam through medieval castles, renaissance art, and baroque architecture as you traverse the pages of this book, immersing yourself in the rich tapestry of Lithuania's architectural heritage.

+ Unveil the Artistic Treasures: Experience the Lithuanian Renaissance through the eyes of renowned artists and delve into the world of Lithuanian literature, music, and dance that continue to inspire and captivate.

+ Savor the Flavors: Embark on a culinary adventure as you explore Lithuanian cuisine, renowned for its hearty and flavorful dishes. From traditional delights to mouthwatering desserts, discover the culinary wonders of this European nation.

+ Embrace Nature's Beauty: Escape to Lithuania's natural wonders, from the enchanting Curonian Spit to the serene national parks and the iconic Hill of Crosses. Experience the serene landscapes that define this Baltic paradise.

+ Preserve the Language: Explore the resilience of the Lithuanian language and its unique alphabet, pronunciation, and linguistic features. Learn about language revival efforts that have kept this ancient tongue alive.

+ Celebrate Traditions: Immerse yourself in the vibrant world of Lithuanian festivals and celebrations, from ancient rituals to modern-day festivities that showcase the spirit and warmth of the Lithuanian people.

+ Experience Lithuanian Hospitality: Uncover the essence of Lithuanian hospitality as you learn about the importance of family, cultural traditions, and the warm welcome that awaits travelers in this charming nation.

+ Souvenirs and Craft Markets: Discover unique Lithuanian souvenirs and craft markets where you can find the perfect memento to remember your journey through this captivating land.

"Lithuania: Everything You Need to Know" is a text-only masterpiece that takes you on a profound journey into the heart of Lithuania. Whether you're an armchair traveler or planning your own adventure, this book is your key to unlocking the wonders of Lithuania, making it an essential addition to your reading collection. Buy your copy today and embark on an unforgettable literary voyage through the beauty of Lithuania!

ISBN 9798865120247

9 798865 120247

90000